HOLDING ON LOOSELY

Opening My Hands, Lightening My Load,
and Seeing Something Else

By
DANA KNOX WRIGHT

Carpenter's Son Publishing

Holding on Loosely: Opening My Hands, Lightening
My Load, and Seeing Something Else

© 2021 by Dana Knox Wright

Published by Clovercroft Publishing, Franklin, Tennessee

Published in association with Larry Carpenter of Christian Book Services, LLC
www.christianbookservices.com

Edited by Tiarra Tompkins

Copy Edit by David Brown

Cover and Interior Design by Suzanne Lawing

Cover illustration by Chyna Mason

Author photo by Austin Pro Photo

Printed in the United States of America

978-1-952025-58-7

To be sensitive, some names in some stories have been changed.

FOR TODD,

whose feet have remained firmly planted next to mine—
through every winter and spring, every summer and fall
of holding on and turning loose.

AUTHOR'S NOTE

I can't remember a time when I didn't cling. It seems I'm hardwired for it. It's made change—most any kind of change—all the more difficult. It's made me hardheaded when I needed to learn a lesson, and trust me, I've needed to learn many.

I've clung to my children when they asked for my blessing to go. I've latched on to someone else's ideas without trusting my own convictions. I've held tightly to my self-righteousness and pride when brought face to face with differences and things I don't understand. Sometimes, I held more tightly to the things I had than the faith I had. I've held on to prejudice when I would tell you I didn't. There've been times I've clung to fear with all my might and it has shut me down for days at a time; and seasons when my busyness kept me from seeing the most meaningful things happening around me. My holding on has kept me lazy and cemented in my comfort zone. It's made me stingy with my time, generous with my expectations, and struggling to let go of my need to please. Clinging has made me impatient and desperate to remain relevant as I age.

This is my history of holding on and these are my stories of turning loose. Sometimes they broke my heart, sometimes they made me laugh, but they always made me see something else. They always freed me—making me better for letting go.

It's the rhythm of all of these stories. They're stories of living minimally, from the inside out.

This book could not have been written in my twenties or my thirties. Nor could it have been written in my forties. The theme of the book required me to live out and write about a good portion of my life before seeing the connectivity in the individual stories—some of which I'd written a long time ago. I wrote many of these stories, or at least a version of them, to stand alone. Turns out they were actually meant to be part of a whole. So, I find myself here at the point of release, slightly nervous to show you so much of me. Even still, I'll open my hands and turn loose of one more thing.

Dana Knox Wright

CONTENTS

PROLOGUE

When I was thirteen, I wanted to marry Donny Osmond. *Tiger Beat Magazine* convinced me it was a possibility. Then, one day in the stands at a basketball game, a boy named Jerry called me "Shirley Pimple", and just like that, I turned loose of my dream of being Mrs. Osmond. Clear skin or not, it likely wouldn't have worked out anyway, being I'm not Mormon.

My mantra then became the lyrics to Janis Ian's only hit song, "Seventeen," where she lamented that the world was designed for the pretty girls with pretty complexions—the ones who got a free pass to the easy life because of it. The song was a self-disparaging anthem, and teens with poor self-image latched on to it like a calf to a teat.

When I was fifteen, I wanted to sing the song in the choir's spring program, but Mr. Richardson wouldn't have it. He said it was a depressing message. In hindsight, I agree. God bless all the educators who got tangled up in my adolescence and had to see my clumsy coming of age. Eventually, I quit buying *Tiger Beat* and listening to Janis Ian, and began filling my bedroom walls with posters of lovely, inspiring words like these:

If you love something, set it free. If it comes back to you, it's yours. If it doesn't, it never was. It's a quote from the novella *Jonathan Livingston Seagull,* by Richard Bach.

The words were handy to fall back on when life got dramatic and just downright crummy. Like when a boyfriend broke up with me. Or when a friend got mad at me and didn't want to be friends anymore. The words brought me some comfort in those teen years.

These pages have fallen into place after revisiting my writings from the last many years. In most all of them, there was a common thread—a wrestling at the ground level. A sort of jockeying for position in my need to possess. To keep. To hold tightly. To control. To label things as mine.

What am I, a three-year-old?

I have followed Jesus for so long, and yet regarding *this* thing— this holding on—I've conducted myself completely contrary to his example.

In these pages are stories of the constant, gentle, humorous, and sometimes firm way I've been led to pry my fingers away from people and places—things, ideas, and attitudes I've held too tightly. These are my lessons in unhanding.

The only part of my old favorite quote that speaks to me at all now is *let it go*. Not *if you love something*. Not because *it will come back to you*.

Simply let it go. That's all.

Life—from its very first breath—looks like this. Hold. Unhand. Repeat.

I'm trying really hard not to resist it.

Chapter 1

THE WHISTLE

Turning Loose of Hard Stuff

There's a way we walk when life is hard. The effort to simply put one foot in front of the other is almost too much—like our feet were set in concrete as we slept. Our steps seem very deliberate—and they are, because the brain is pulling every bribe out of its bag of tricks to get us to keep moving.

No one can dodge these seasons. I can't think of a single one who has.

Some of us have the ability to move through them still smiling, and others of us can hardly pull ourselves out of bed. Some of us ease the pain by talking about it to everyone we know, as if we can talk it into passing more quickly. Others of us want to hide under our favorite blanket until we get the all clear, which we're not sure will ever come.

I'm the latter of the two, which is not surprising since I always loved a good tent when I was a kid. Oh, I'm a hider from way back—the neighborhood hide-and-seek champion.

A dear friend of mine responds to hard stuff like this. She runs away from it. *Literally.* If something happens in the front of a room, she runs to the back of the room, where she refuses to look the hard thing in the eye until she takes a minute to process it. Then, when she's ready, she calmly turns and faces it.

We all have our own ways, I suppose.

Sometimes, hard stuff comes in fast—knocking the breath out of us because we never saw it coming. For me, though, it wasn't the way it came. My hardest season to date came in slowly—easing its way into my sanctuary of home and my sanctuary of heart, stealing bits of me a little at a time. It was a sly creature, and it was unmerciful as it toyed with emotions that grew ever more brittle with the duration of its stay.

Then one day, it reached its full potential, and it was ugly.

UGLY.

It was an economy thing—a money thing. And at the end of the day, we didn't have any. That's the long and short of it anyway. It was 2008, and almost everyone in the country was struggling in some way. All I could see, though, was the struggle right in front of me. *My* struggle. To sum it up like this seems so matter-of-fact now, told with hardly any emotion at all. The truth is, though, even now I can't open the door to it for fear it will all come crashing in on me again. My pulse is speeding up as I type. In between every line I've written are gallons of tears, one thousand sleepless nights, and countless pleas to God. Before it all hit the fan, we were a couple of kids, my husband and I, with kids of our own—living a good life, leading out in our church, and too busy, optimistic, and naive to see the knots beginning to fray. And even when it started to come to light, my husband tried hard to protect me from the ugliness of it. He tried to fix it before it hurt me.

There were many things my husband and I didn't know about each other when we married at the ridiculously infantile age of twenty-one.

I didn't know he was an award-winning procrastinator. I didn't know he would use a bath towel for an entire month if I didn't put it in the hamper and lay out a fresh one for him. I didn't know he would surprise me often with flowers, while never remembering which were my favorites.

It wasn't a walk in the park for him, either. He didn't know I often wash the sheets and forget to put them back on the bed until it's bedtime, or how I can't go to sleep without a smidge of Vicks VapoRub under my nose. He didn't know how seriously I despise clutter in every form and fashion, and how I like to arrive everywhere a good thirty minutes early. He didn't know I could hang on to a good mad for as long as forty-eight hours.

The *first* ten years, we hashed these things out with only a little bloodletting.

The *second* ten years, we didn't give a single crap about them because we were busy doing other things.

The *third* ten years we'll forever refer to as The Great Humbling. It was when the rubber met the road of the *big* things, and we forgot all about the small things. In fact, we *longed* for the days of small things. Even after all the years of marriage, we each wondered how the other would fare against formidable, joy-sucking bottom dwellers intent on moving in with us.

Things went away right and left—some by choice, and some otherwise. Some needed to go away and I knew it, but I still held tightly, only making their extraction from my hands all the more excruciating. I was a spoiled child, stamping my foot and screaming *mine*.

The mortgage industry was in shambles and my husband's work went away overnight. We were almost fifty years old and suddenly, we couldn't pay our bills. Cars went back to the dealership, and we drove a truck borrowed from a friend. Our cell phone service was suspended. We reverted to eating like we did in college—lots of pasta. Our home was under the threat of foreclosure for almost two years, and I hid inside, peering out the window anytime I heard a dog bark— afraid someone would show up and make me leave. Of course, a reasonable person would know that isn't the way things go down, but fear did something strange to me. It made me scared and suspicious and paranoid. I was afraid to check the mail—afraid to look at the notices that were being sent. Once, my mother's neighbor asked her how we were doing because she'd heard we were losing our home, and from that moment forward, I felt like everyone knew every detail of our circumstance.

The very worst part was we could hide nothing from our children. One of our sons was stranded at a school in a foreign country and we couldn't pay tuition. Really, *that* was the worst part of it—our children seeing and knowing the things we didn't want them to see and know. I know it's flawed thinking *now*, but *then* it was gut-wrenching to have them see us flounder and fail—to see we weren't holding any piece of it together.

Most days, I was a mess. Really most *every* day.

The thing about living in a small town when you go through life's hard stuff is you feel like you're going through it with an audience. I'd watched others go through it—sometimes their brand of suffering made the front page of the local paper. Mine wasn't like that, but if you heard a whisper of it and *wanted* to see, you wouldn't have to look far. I was full of pride, full of humiliation, and full of sadness. I talked to no one in town about it. I was the opposite of transparent. See, I told you. I'm a hider.

When hard stuff reached its climax—when we could see no options in front of us—things in the house went quiet for a while. It was like sunshine left. The piano sitting in our living room fell silent because to play it required energy I didn't have. There was, of course, the *obvious* reason for it, but there was something else I couldn't put my finger on.

Something gone.

Something I didn't miss, until it came back to me one day.

It was still dark as I lay in bed, dreading the arrival of another day of struggles. I heard hushed morning noises and pictured exactly where my husband was. His morning customs were as familiar to me as my own right hand. I knew he'd be sitting on the couch in our living room, listening to God—or maybe even on his knees, where I'd found him in other desperate times. For years, it had been his way. Soon, I heard him move into the kitchen to get the coffee going.

Then out of the quiet, my husband began to whistle.

At first, it seemed strange and out of place to me in a house gone dreary. But as he continued to whistle, something in me sparked. It's hard to resist a whistle.

On that morning, a silly little whistle was hope wrapped up just for me—it was the thing gone missing—actually the thing representing an entire subset of other happy things gone missing—things I'd dismissed so I could wallow in the mess. They all seemed to rush back to me in that moment. I felt like I was sucking in air after being underwater too long. This small thing of a whistle, after I'd unhanded so many large things, had the power to push me back toward joy and life that morning. It was good medicine. It was a life raft tossed to me in an angry ocean. It was relief, amplified, and oh so welcomed.

It is well tears are different from *plain old* tears, and I cried a bucket of them that morning because I knew in the deepest part of me I could survive losing many things, but I could never survive losing my husband's whistle—the placeholder for everything most precious to me. The whistle signaled to me the beginning of their return.

It's when I let go. I opened up my hands and began to let things be what they would be. It was a strange kind of freedom because nothing in our situation was changed, but still everything had changed.

I'd forgotten who I was for a while, but I began to remember. Very soon, I stopped crying about it all. I got up. I wiped my eyes. I put on some makeup and I felt a little of me start to come back. When I put on my tennis shoes and got my hands dirty, I recognized myself in the mirror. I'd missed me.

Getting my hands dirty looked like this.

Out of necessity, I considered all of my well-curated possessions and I separated them into two piles—things needed and things wanted.

Oh, the things *wanted*. I'd filled my home with them over the years—pretty things, rare things, and old things. Because I loved collections, *things* in my house accumulated. Collections of clocks on shelves. Old books with meaningful titles. Goofus glass plates and bowls. Armoires. Random old chairs because one can't have too many of those. Vintage linens. I promise you this is nowhere near an exhaustive list. I've never liked clutter though, so I was tidy about it. Still, it was a profusion of whatnots. It was an explosion of treasure, filling the storehouse to the brim. I hunted for them when I was happy and I hunted when I was sad. I hunted when I was stressed out, too busy, and obsessively dieting. Truthfully, I was a forty-something hunter-gatherer-keeper. I thought it was the undeniable antidote for every range of emotion in me, and I was good at it.

These were the *wanted* things I sold to put food on the table and pay bills—several thousand dollars of *wanted* things. I called all the people I knew who bought and sold old things and I invited them over. I had myself a sale to end all sales, though not one of them knew the real reason I was selling everything. At the end of the day, most all of my treasures went to live with other people and I've never missed a single one of them for a second. Because on the day I let them go, they didn't even look like treasures anymore. They looked like deliverance. Like a rescue. Like freedom. It was the miracle of turning things loose.

I was forty-nine years old when I became acquainted with the gift of enough, courtesy of The Great Humbling.

I was getting stronger by the minute.

The hard stuff was far from over, but I was suited up for the rest of the battle. Work and money were still scarce, but we were on track again—with my husband and I teaming up to turn things around. Gradually, *hard* became *challenging*. *Challenging* became *doable*. And *doable* finally became *done*. It took a while. Who am I kidding? It took *years*. But hear me say this:

We are elastic. We bounce back.

We're still here and we're okay. Honestly, we're *better* than okay because God doesn't abandon us in the hard stuff. Not you and not me. He doesn't give us over to it, even when we're ready to give up the fight. Not ever. Not even one time. God's steadfastness is in the ink in every line of our stories. Oddly enough, a silly little whistle pulled me out of the deep. When the water receded, my rain boots came off and I ran barefoot again.

One year when school was out, long before the Great Humbling, we moved our family from the city to the country. While our house was being renovated, we lived on a lake for the summer. We unpacked just enough—dishes for the five of us, bikes for the kids, a few games, and one family picture. We had a television equipped only to play VHS tapes. We slept, swam, fished, ate, napped, and that's all. We hardly unpacked any possessions and we didn't miss a single one of them. I recently asked each of my children to tell me which was their favorite summer as a kid. Each one said, without hesitation, that summer.

The summer without stuff.

There's a tipping point when it comes to possessions. When we reach the point of *enough*, everything after it actually gives us diminishing returns. It binds us up, whets our appetite for *more*, and actually steals away our attention from the place of real peace—where real contentment lives. *More* is not *more*. *More* is *less*.

From time to time, I think about the hard stuff, and even the memory of it stirs up the old familiar tightening in my gut, and I have to turn it loose. Again and again. Every time. I have to lay it on the table in front of me and walk the other way.

What started as a *necessity* to get rid of possessions became a *desire* in me to let go of things. Even when I stood in the light at the end of The Great Humbling tunnel, the compulsion to possess did not return and the yearning to let go did not leave.

It has since become my joy to give things away. Turning loose of things has become my favorite sport. And not just things I *no longer* love, but things I *currently* love. I am telling you, I loved my old milk glass pitcher—the one with the red polka dots. It was one of the few treasures I held on to in The Great Humbling. I couldn't have known when I kept it that the *most* joy it would bring me would be not in *having* it, but in letting it go when I gave it to a friend who loved it too. It is sheer delight to love something for a season and pass it on. Hold and release.

When my father died, the only thing I asked my mother for was his coffee cup—the one I'd watched him drink from since I was a little girl. I wasn't sure she'd let go of it, but she did. It was precious to me, and I would drink from it on days I needed to feel him near. One day, my grown son asked if he could have it. I thought how easily my mother released it to me as I handed it to him. It was his turn with it. Now, *he* drinks from it and thinks of his grandfather.

The real value of a mere thing lies not in it sitting stationary on a shelf, only to look pretty. Its value is in its ability to bring cheer when it passes from me to you. There is a time to hold and a time to turn loose of just about everything.

I still love living in a well-cultivated pretty space. It's a different space than where we lived through the hard stuff. That place finally sold, and that too was a gift in the end. It doesn't take much, I've learned. Aesthetics make me happy. I rarely sit down to write without lighting a candle near me. I love fresh flowers in a pretty, chipped vase next to a collection of carefully placed little books. That said, if you ask me if you can have them, I will say yes. I wouldn't always have said yes, but I will now. Because I have enough. I'm smiling as I write these words, knowing I mean them all the way down to my soul.

Of all the unhandings I've written about—the tangible ones and the intangible ones—the turning loose of possessions feels the most permanent to me. It's the one I feel most settled about—the one requiring few reminders. It's the one that gave me almost immediate relief. My head and my heart don't have to jockey for position on this one. Both of them feel right about it—about giving away, emptying the storehouse, and really and truly not wanting more.

The Great Humbling was equal parts mess and beauty, though I didn't see any evidence of beauty when I was living it. Now though, I clearly see it was the beginning of seeing something else. It was liberating in ways I could never have imagined. It propelled me to head off in the direction of other things needing to be loosed. In fact, I was scouting for them. And they were everywhere.

Chapter 2

THE BEST PARTS OF ME

Turning Loose of My Children

Who can understand the urge to hitch a ride across Bolivia in the back of a truck full of chickens or the desire to bike with a brother fifteen hundred miles through four countries? Where does a passion to wander come from—the beckoning kind of passion, pulling souls like magnets across unsafe borders? What inner thing moves a girl, so newly considered an adult she really isn't one, to abandon education to travel to places far—to work on a Swedish horse farm and write songs beneath the shadow of a windmill? Who can understand the pull on a heart to leave behind what's known and safe to go far? What gap begs to be filled not by a faith taught, but by a faith found? Who can understand any of this, apart from the one who craves it?

I'll tell you who can understand it. The mother who turned them loose *for* it. But before I could understand it, there was this.

I was blissfully naïve at the things to come one March morning when the grandest surprise came to me in the shape of an eight-and-a-half-pound boy—a swaddled roll of a baby with a mess of the darkest black hair. No early sonogram to spoil our surprise. No gender-reveal party. Just the truest, most meaningful surprise a grown-up could get—and I use the word *grown-up* ever so loosely. I was twenty-four and clueless to the ways of mothering.

There's this thing my heart did when I held a fresh-from-the-womb human being for the first time—a human being who grew inside me—one I would instinctively nurture and protect for the rest of my life. There aren't words to describe this particular kind of joy.

He was the first of mine to do everything.

First to sleep through the night. First to cut a tooth, and first to *lose* a tooth.

The first to throw up on me on an airplane. The first to walk, to fly a kite, to go fishing, and to catch frogs. The first to ride a bike and the first to ask me to be his princess.

He was the one who made us want others.

This boy was our experiment—for which we've apologized repeatedly. We cut our parenting teeth on him.

I experimented on cutting his hair, on finding ways to get an antibiotic through his clenched teeth, and I experimented with his discipline. Despite all the experimentation, remarkably he lived, with only a single visit to the emergency room requiring a surgical rebuilding of his nasal passage. But that's really about it.

He started saying "bye-bye" before his first birthday, but he meant it in earnest when he was three and left to stay a week with his grandparents. He left with them and never looked back, and I thought I would die. I thought it was the hardest goodbye in the world. I was again naïve—*this* time in the ways goodbyes with our children would go.

When he was five, he said goodbye and walked in Ms. Dickey's classroom. I hid outside the window and watched him be brave. I knew he would figure everything out. *That* goodbye was harder than the one before—easier than the one to follow. It was only the beginning of a long, beautiful, and bittersweet dance with my boy and me.

Then it happened again. And again. Two more times.

Next with a second son—so different from the first in the particular joy he stirred in me. He was the second to do everything—the one in the middle. The quiet thinker. The hysterically funny one. The one who pushed every boundary of protection and safety I laid out for him. A loyal comrade to his big brother. The one whose own name was, and is, the only accurate adjective to describe him. *That's so Jake.*

The third go-round, our surprise was a girl, entering the world large and in charge doling out a particular joy that was right off the bat opinionated and bossy. I knew she'd be strong. She wore bows the size of Texas in her thick strawberry blonde hair and sometimes, we wore matching pajamas—she and I. Even when she brought up the back of the line at preschool, she called herself the leader. She was one-half dreamer and one-half realist … going from fearful to fearless in about a decade.

I held these three tightly in my arms. I held them fiercely in my heart. No matter how I banished the thought from my mind, I knew the releasing had already begun the minute each of them was placed in my arms.

Hold and release.

More holding in the early years, more releasing as each birthday came and went, as if a permanent marker couldn't wait to indelibly mark the passage of time so I could never go back.

At the root of every struggle between my children and me over the years, and there were not many, was simply *my* selfish yearning to hold and direct their lives, and *their* independent spirits straining to be turned loose. I'm thankful it came in bits and pieces and not all at once.

I released them to have overnights. I released them to drive to the city, to date, to go to college, and to travel the world.

Those releases led to others. Harder ones. Ones I tried to manipulate—the way mamas can do. I was so certain I knew best for them. Sometimes, they let me have my way, but sometimes, they pushed back and stood their ground with me. I'm retrospectively proud of them for it.

I released them to face fears, deal with disappointments, and choose their own joy. I released them to make decisions, even when I didn't agree with them. I released them to be strong men—to be a strong woman.

Some turning loose was easier than others. Some of it was so hard, I couldn't look them in the eye at the moment we broke contact and my hand left theirs.

Some of it was physical and some of it was spiritual—best dealt with in the privacy of my heart, long after I had any business, any say, or any right to steer their lives. That releasing was, and is, to God alone.

High on a shelf in a closet downstairs are hidden away six boxes. In them live the very condensed, but real, tangible evidence that I once had three little ones who lived with me. Two boxes per child. Very efficient, I think.

In them are notes written in a kid's hand, thanking me for cooking macaroni and cheese. There are photographs and old guitar strings. There are Beanie Babies and thousands of baseball cards. There are programs from concerts and keepsakes from trips. There are old shot records proving I was a responsible mother. There are children's Bibles and love notes from the kids to us and from us to them.

The truth is, if it wasn't weird, I would still have all their childhood stuff out and about. I would have their trophies on my shelves and their larger-than-life photos on my walls.

But that would be weird. And probably a little pitiful. Desperate even.

So instead, six boxes remembering three childhoods—fifty-four combined years of childhood. Twenty-four years of mothering in my little nest. Fifty-four birthday parties. I watched it all happen. I had a front-row seat.

These boxes are so dear to me because in every treasure, I'm woven into the mix—snapshots of their lives when I was a main character. And I loved it. I loved having a starring role. It was a role I embraced—a role I grew into. Academy Award-winning material.

And that's what's changed. It's what turning loose does.

We don't run in the same circles anymore. Furthermore, though I don't get it, it's likely there are successions of days that pass when I'm not even a thought. Not even a blip on the radar.

It's true and it packs a punch.

Maybe it's why I kept the boxes.

Oh I know, it's how things have to go down, but I still can't speak of it without a lump in my throat the size of a small island.

They had to leave—it was time. They had to have experiences and conversations to which I will never be privy—unless, of course, a sibling slips up and happens to mention something about being robbed at knifepoint one night in Quito (I was never supposed to know about that one).

They have inside jokes I'm not in on, doctor visits of which I will never know the particulars. They have daily routines I know nothing about. I don't know their favorite restaurants, I don't know how much money is in their bank accounts and I mostly have no idea what they're up to tonight. In conversations, they refer to friends I don't know. I am not their go-to confidante anymore.

At one time, I was thankful for social media where I was able to at least get glimpses of the lives my children lead apart from me. But then, they all mostly defected from social media to live more unplugged lives and they went away from me again.

Mothering is a hard habit to break.

It's as if we're supposed to flip a switch the moment they turn eighteen, and just quit it. Quit mothering. In fact, the very things which make us award-winning mothers when they're younger suddenly make us helicopter moms when they're older. It's mean. A cruel trick. Don't try to convince me otherwise.

I will always wish to know the adult versions of them as well as I know the child versions.

As I look at my children from a distance now, as I stand in the cheering section, I see something else. I see others who have come close to them. Wives. Good friends. Co-workers. Their own children. Mentors. A church community. It happened so seamlessly there was never much of a gap or a void in their lives at all. In some strange way, there is great peace and even relief in it for me.

I love the *others* who have come near—the *others* who love them. People near my children are *for* them, and it is the dearest gift to me. My children are the best parts of me, and when I turned loose of them, it gave others the chance to know the joy of them. Lucky them.

Others once included a community of Quechua women. Just out of college, my son worked for a nonprofit providing assistance to people in the Amazon. In case you're wondering, I never saw this one coming. Nor could I have imagined one day he would be terribly sick in a jungle in Ecuador and native women would stand in the gap for me and make him well by pouring a concoction of sorts up his nose. In my wildest dreams, I couldn't have imagined it. They mothered him when I could not. They made him well. Provision comes in the most beautiful ways.

Sometimes they're close, and sometimes they're oceans away, my three. Sometimes I know vaguely, but not *exactly*, where they are on the planet.

But I'll be here. I'll be the keeper of the boxes.

Boxes that mean much more to me than to my kids. To think one day they'll want them is wishful thinking. One day, they'll look through them and laugh and be nostalgic for half a second, but these remnants of their childhood won't tug at their hearts like they tug at mine. I'm fairly certain they won't and it's okay.

On their own and with no help from me, they've added wonderful new layers to who they are. They are fully themselves, still with a bit of me coursing through their veins. It's enough and it's everything, as I continue to figure out who *I* am apart from them. My greatest discovery in all of this is the understanding it's possible to remain close to each other even when we're miles apart. This is not a sad story. It's the grandest story of watching my children rise—watching them stand. I've lived a thousand adventures through the words they've written to me over the years.

> *August 2007*
> *Dear Mom and Dad,*
> *Even though you think I'm too old for you to tell me what I can and can't do, I still want to thank you for letting me go. It wouldn't mean nearly as much and would be much more difficult without your blessing. Your support means so much. I couldn't do this without you guys. I love and miss you.*

> *December 2008*
> *Hey! Things are good here as we finally got going with our little projects in the two communities outside of San Cristobal this week. In one community we'll be working at a school twice a week teaching English and planting a garden with them. In the other community I am helping with a project that will eventually offer nutrition classes. Out of all the places I've been abroad, I could see myself staying here the longest. It's such a cool little town! I wish y'all could come.*
> *I miss and love you all,*

> *June 2018*
> *Hey! It's 4am in the lovely village of Harlosa, Sweden and I can't sleep. After lying in bed for a couple hours forcing my eyes closed, I decided to yield to the power of jet lag and to make use of my wide-awake brain. I now finally have the space to consider things that have been sitting just under the surface for a very long time.*
> *Talk soon,*

In holding my three and turning loose of them, they taught me about everything that really matters. They opened up the world to me and helped me to see things through fresh eyes. They made me curious. They challenged me to live a life of adventure and to keep moving. Our conversations are fresh and deep and interesting. Our hugs are long, our goodbyes still hard, but our hellos are glorious.

This day, and most every other happy day, is and was brought to me in part by these three—these three who are both known and unknown to me.

Mine and yet not mine.

One time when I was lonely for them, I questioned my turning loose so completely. I was sad for the occasional birthdays and holidays we didn't spend together. I was sad because they didn't seem quite as sad about it as I was. I compared my story with others—I compared my children to theirs. I did it for half a minute, before I stopped myself. I don't recommend it. It's never comparing apples to apples.

Then I heard a sermon about a quiver full of arrows—arrows meant to fly—and those words were a healing balm. They were truth to me.

My story of being a mama is this.

I held my sons and daughter for my allotted time—the most beautiful time—and with the greatest expression of love and trust and confidence I could bestow upon them, I released them. Their unhanding remains the most beautiful, the most terrifying, and the most sacred letting go of them all.

It's the fullest and dearest way this mama knew to love these children.

The deepest of all love lets go.

It then flies to a comfortable little perch where it remains always just within reach.

Chapter 3

THE PEOPLE OF ECONOMY

Turning Loose of Pretension

My earliest recollection of airplanes and airports was when my grandparents flew in from across the ocean where they lived and worked. Twice a year, we would pick them up at the airport. They'd visit for a couple of months and then we'd see them off again. It was before crazy security risks, so we could walk right up to the gate with them. Jet bridges didn't exist, so they walked downstairs and directly onto the tarmac. As they made their way to the plane, my grandmother would turn every few steps to wave to us, three little girls with noses pressed against the glass—romanticizing over the fanciness of air travel.

Air travel in the 1960s and 1970s was nothing like it is today. Women wore pantyhose instead of compression socks, heels instead of tennis shoes. Everyone dressed to the nines, even for long flights— inspired by the President and First Lady flying Air Force One.

So it isn't surprising it was my grandmother who took me on my first airplane trip when I was eleven years old. It was 1971 and we were flying from Alexandria, Louisiana to Lubbock, Texas, but I felt like we were going to Paris, France. We flew Delta. She gave me the window seat and I felt so fancy. Almost none of my friends in my small Texas town had ever flown and I felt like I was famous.

To this day, I still feel fancy when I step through the doors into an airport. I do, even though it seems ridiculous. I've purchased many of the essentials for air travel done classy—a comfortable, wrinkle-free travel top and leggings, practical but stylish shoes for rushing to make a connection, and a great leather bag for stowing all my travel sundries. But the cold hard truth is this. If fancy is as fancy does, my flying history will not lie. It always finds me out, because I cannot pull off being chic in any form, including on an airplane.

I took an early-morning flight years ago with my firstborn infant son. We looked so adorable, the two of us. I had visions of landing and being met by adoring family members—all of them wondering how I managed to have it all so together. Then, in all our pre-boarding glory, we were halfway down the jet bridge when he full-on projectile vomited on the both of us. I couldn't turn back. I could only continue on. *Who are you impressing now, Ms. Fancypants?* A few years later, I made my first trip to L.A. with my husband for business. I was going to Hollywood! I thought I was so classy with my permed hair and my cute maternity dress—both homemade and compliments of my dear mother-in-law. Pictures don't lie, though, and I've seen them. I wasn't posh at all. Nope. I was *Rebecca of Sunnybrook Farm* come to town. On a plane.

See what I mean?

It was a red-letter day the first time I flew on a plane that wasn't booked to capacity. I couldn't believe my luck to land a spot on a half-full plane. And it wasn't just me. Everyone in economy was over-the-top excited!

What? You mean no one has to sit in the gosh-awful torture chamber that is the middle seat?

Once the flight attendant announced boarding was complete, everyone shifted about the cabin, running to and fro as if we were children on an Easter egg hunt. We all spread out, desperate to relish the unexpected gift of space.

My husband and I put a seat between us just because we could. A woman came charging up from the back and found a row all to herself. She was absolutely giddy as she waved to her people in the back of the plane, giving them the thumbs-up as if to say, *look at me! Isn't this just the best day ever?*

And for the next one-and-a-half hours from Charlotte to Indianapolis, we all felt like we were in first class. Why, I have never seen such joy on a plane.

So, this is what it feels like to fly the friendly skies, I thought. At last, I understood the slogan.

Oh, we all knew it wouldn't last forever. Trust me. We all know who we are.

We are the people of economy, and it usually goes like this:

Usually, the flight is oversold, and we're asked to volunteer to give up our seat for a free seat on the next flight out. *So generous.* I mean, since we really have nowhere to be. Then we're hit with the truth there might not be enough overhead space for our carry-ons.

The boarding begins. Right after those who need assistance and people with small children board the plane, the first-class fliers are next in line—Group One Priority is printed on their boarding passes.

When those in Group One Priority approach the airline agent before entering the jet bridge, they are the relaxed and laughing ones—with stylish carry-ons that never seem to have wonky rollers, duct-taped zippers, or pull-up handles that get stuck halfway. They seem to travel light and organized—their coffee of choice in hand. The next time I see them is when I parade past them on my way to the bowels of economy. They're still smiling. Believe me when I say I'm not judging them. Truth is, I really want to *be* them—sipping a nice Syrah.

Sometimes, when I'm in Boarding Group Seven, the economy line is backed up all the way into first class and it's at a standstill. This is likely the most unpleasant part of first class flying—the boarding of *the rest.* I get it because this is when economy children begin to wail, and their parents begin to sweat.

They sweat because in three-two-one, their kid will launch his paci. Dad's eyes will dart about frantically trying to find where it landed as his child begins to wail. There it is, just under the first class lady's chair. Dad will bend down to retrieve the paci, aware he has totally invaded the lady's personal space. He will attempt a quick getaway, but instead, he will practically take her out with the heavy diaper bag as it slips off his shoulder. Coffee will spill. Poor her. Poor him. Everyone's a loser.

Excuse me. So sorry—it will be all the poor, red-faced dad can say as he plugs up the child with the dirty paci.

All forward momentum ceases because a hunt is going on in economy—a hunt for storage space in the overhead bins. We were duly warned this might happen.

Here's the thing. No matter how carefully we packed our liquids in small, 3.4-ounce containers or how hard we worked to squeeze them in a quart-size clear plastic bag for easy screening by the scary screening guys who never smile, it doesn't matter. Here is our likely reality. We're probably going to drag our roly bags down that skinny little aisle, only to discover our $500 round-trip ticket did not buy us overhead bin space. Let me say one cannot feel fancy dragging a roly bag back up the aisle. *Excuse me. Oh, pardon me. Sorry sir, if I could just squeeze by again.*

We flew Premium Economy once because it was our first intercontinental flight and we thought we could use a little leg room to reduce our risk of blood clots. The seats were right behind the bulkhead wall, just steps from First Class.

The extra room was nice, I'll admit, and there was no middle seat situation to deal with—just our two seats on one side of the plane. *This is basically first class,* I told myself, smoothing my well-thought-out travel clothes and feeling slightly fancy. It was right before the flight attendant pulled the curtain between economy and first class and said even though we were mere steps from the restrooms just on the other side of that curtain, we would need to use the ones at the back of the plane. *The economy ones.*

Legalism.

We are rule followers, my husband and I, so we complied—despite the reality of "going" problems that come with being middle-aged.

Mealtime.

Which Lunchable-type adult meal did I want? Neither. Exactly neither. I chose the vegetarian, though, because it seemed less fake. I couldn't risk the whole *hangry* thing. If one gets in trouble over the Atlantic and she's already in economy, what then? Where is she banished to then?

The curtain separating us from first class was a see-through gray mesh. It's mean-spirited, I think, because it teases those of us in economy. I asked my husband if he could see first class. He leaned out into the aisle a bit and took a peek. Yes, he told me. He could see.

Tell me everything, I said. *Tell me. I can handle it.*

A garden fresh salad. It's what he saw a woman eating! It was served in a lovely white ceramic bowl with real utensils. Her wine was served in a real wine glass. *Lucky her,* I thought as I breathed deeply and peeled back the plastic cover on my veggie plate. I was halfway finished with the slightly rubbery broccoli when I broke a tine off my plastic spork.

Bedtime.

There is really no bedtime in economy. There are only naps. Naps until butts go numb, knees ache, necks get cricks, and bladders get full. Lights going on and off all night long. There are attempts to read, to sleep, to watch a movie, and finally pleas to God to show mercy and let daylight come. Repeat.

I should not let my eyes wander outside economy. I learn good things when I look at others like me—when I observe their economy coping skills.

Take my neighbor across the aisle, for instance. He had international travel down to an art. He took his bag and headed to the back of the plane—I assumed to the bathroom. He returned in house shoes and pajama bottoms. He used his carry-on as a sort of footrest, plugged in his earbuds, tucked the scrawny little blanket tightly around him, and promptly drifted off into sleepy land, happy as a clam.

We the people of economy. Headed to Europe.

I'm mostly not headed to Europe though—usually just taking a relatively short flight in the states. Sometimes, we land the absolute last seats on the back of the plane because we didn't pick our seats for an upcharge. Boarding Group 1,023. Row *there-are-no-more-rows*. It's like being in time-out at thirty-five thousand feet. The seats don't recline on the last row, but lucky for the Jersey Girl in front of me, hers does recline. Her head of dark, thick hair so close to me that when I breathe, her hair blows in the breeze. She talks loudly and incessantly. She talks to her friends two rows up and across the aisle. They pass each other carrots and hummus. I would not lie to you. I can't make this stuff up.

The people of economy.

Sometimes, there's a sick, hacking guy on the row in front of me. He's thoughtful, though. He wears a black hoodie pulled up for the entire flight. He makes me a little nervous despite his illness. I am at the same time thankful for security screening and ashamed for pro-filing him.

Dude. Really sorry. Sometimes, I wear hoodies too. Feel better.

We are the people of economy.

We are gray hairs, green hairs, pink hairs, and purple hairs. And baldheads. We are single moms who sometimes smell like throw-up, and businesspeople who need to close a deal. We are retired folks and families on vacation. We're sometimes well behaved and sometimes, we're an unruly sort. Sometimes, grateful flight attendants sneak us cute little bottles of whiskey for exhibiting good and patient behavior. Other times, we need a good tasing.

In the end, it all boils down to this: We are not grand people back here. We pretended for half a second that flying made us kind of fancy, but it doesn't. We've collectively turned loose of every ounce of pretension. We're all just who we are and we're trying to be okay with it, one miserable flight at a time. Still, we're a *thankful* people, the people of economy—or at least we will be once we make it *off the stinking plane.*

Chapter 4

THE ZINNIA

Turning Loose of Drought

I was raised in a west Texas desert, where most everything is colored brown and covered in a layer of dust. Dust is just a nice word for dirt. Dirt was everywhere. Girls wore dresses to school when I was a kid, and recess could be torture—blowing dirt can pack quite a sting to bare legs.

I live in a greener place now, and by *now*, I mean for most of the year it's a greener place—with trees and water and grass. I don't mean *now* now though—not August. In August, I'm in a desert again—and this year we're in a full-blown drought. Water wells are going dry right and left. The river barely has the energy to run at all. Me neither. Tap water is never cooler than lukewarm. Our water is rationed.

Every day is mostly the same in August. Triple digits. Sunny, with no chance of rain. It's suffocating and every year, I feel like it is never going to end. Kind of like pregnancy. My head knows it will end, but my heart feels like it won't. It's my August temperament.

So in the midst of August, there was outdoor work to be done. The very moment the sun offered the tiniest bit of light, I went outside.

The only thing on my mind was getting the job done before the heat settled in and before I could talk myself out of it. Oh make no mistake, I was going to sweat either way, because in Texas in the month of August, to breathe is to sweat.

On my porch that morning—a porch fully exposed to long, sunny days—there were twenty-one pots of various sizes. Eleven of those pots held dead things. I have to say, I did all I could to will them to live, but in the end, they just didn't want to live another day on that hot porch. Not the tomatoes. Not the rosemary. Not the lavender. I tried to convince the tomatoes if they'd hold on a few more months, they'd thrive again in the fall. They refused. I told the rosemary she was my favorite garnish ever, but I don't think she believed me. Clearly, it was a one-sided relationship.

So that morning, my job was the removal of dead things.

It took me less than thirty minutes to pull them, bag them, and sweep up the residual mess. As I watered the few things that still had some desire to live, I fixed my attention on a lone zinnia that somehow found its way into a large pot holding an Italian cypress tree. Zinnias are my favorite, and I easily grow a crop of them every year. That year, however, they failed.

Except for the one.

I noticed her as soon as she sprung up green through the soil in a pot where she didn't belong. I didn't let her know I was watching. Weeks before, I'd pulled her uncooperative relatives from their pots when they failed me, thinking she would likely soon follow their lead.

Instead, she thrived. Amidst pots of dead things and prickly cactus, she produced the most beautiful orange bloom. On my porch, she's the clear winner—the belle of the ball—encouraging the other growing things to hang on. She wasn't just pretty—she was tenacious. She didn't cling to the drought, as I am prone to do. She toughed it out, knowing fall would come and blooming wouldn't be so hard anymore.

I think of seasons of drought in my own life. There was a time when I sat down and said, *Okay, you win. Have your way with me. I'm done.*

Looking back, I see clearly I chose it. I grabbed its hand because it was easier as I gave up the fight. I let myself become parched and cracked, and I closed my eyes to the opportunity to stand and to see things through. I was without courage.

Turning loose of drought looks the complete opposite.

I've learned to keep walking in dry seasons. In monotonous seasons. In uncertain seasons. In life and death seasons. I learned it from seeing something—seeing my friend in her season of drought.

Not very long ago, she had a really bad year. One hard thing would have just resolved itself when another hard thing would happen. Relief was little more than a breath between gasps. Each time, I would say to God, *Oh come on! That's enough!*

While I was being impatient with God on her behalf, she was simply asking him to make all of it count for something. She was unhanding drought. Over and over, she did it. She stripped it of all its power.

We can cling to the drought and let it do us in, or we can turn it loose and strengthen our resolve to make it through, knowing God will not leave us there. Droughts don't last forever. They always end with abundant rainfall—rehydrating everything gone dry.

 *Chapter 5*

DESPERATION

Turning Loose of a Paradigm

I am insulated. I know it.

I live in a mostly pretty world.

Images that aren't nice or pretty and don't personally touch me are relegated to the back of my mind—to a room I don't visit often—where I keep the door closed. See, if I can keep ugly things behind that door, then it's like they don't exist at all.

Oh, but they do.

One day, they came close and the air around me changed. My heart began to beat faster and I could taste the smallest bit of fear on my tongue.

I remember the exact moment desperation came close, picking away at the insulation I'd wrapped around me. It changed me. It was unlike any desperation I have known, though I admit to having known only a little. It was the moment when I changed my mind, and in so doing, turned loose of a paradigm.

When a child is born, a mother is born. There's no extracting the person she was before because she no longer exists. On the outside, she looks the same, but on the inside, there's something new running through her veins. She's a new being called by a new name.

Mom. Mama. Mother.

Madre. Ummi. Mum.

Moeder. Morsa. Mueter. Mami.

No matter where she is in this world or what kind of ground is beneath her feet—dirt, grass, concrete, mud, or sand—she will lay her life down on that ground to protect her babies. She will say goodbye to them, though it will grieve her until the day she dies, if it means they will be safe and have something better. She will make unimaginable sacrifices and choices because she loves them. She will swallow her own fear on a daily basis to fill them with the courage they need for the day ahead.

I know this because I am one. I know others. We are her.

I know this because I went way down south once, and what I saw, I'll never un-see—what I heard, I'll never forget.

It was with a bit of trepidation I traveled to a Texas border town. I packed up boxes of a book I wrote and I headed out on a six-hour drive to a place where I was invited to read to school children—a small town in the Rio Grande Valley. I went through a checkpoint to get there, and I nervously answered all the questions. Checkpoints make everyone nervous, I think.

There were five elementary schools in the little town—all of them were needed to accommodate the growing number of Mexican children attending school in the U.S. Many of them are U.S. citizens living in Mexico because their parents aren't citizens and have been deported—likely more than once.

These beautiful children wake early—before daylight—to make the trek across the international bridge to attend school. The days I visited their schools, they came with backpacks and sack lunches. They came with neat and clean hair, braided and tied with bows. The little boys have a clear affinity for hair products. They were tidy, and I knew a mother was behind it. They called me *Miss* and giggled at me—the anomaly with fair skin and blond hair.

Those beautiful, outer coverings of the children I could easily see, but there were things they carried inside them I couldn't see.

I was told that every day, some children came with stories they only whisper to school counselors behind closed doors. In the week I was their guest, those counselors whispered stories to me. Stories with no names, whispered because the fear of retaliation is very real in border towns.

These babies have mamas, I kept thinking—mothers who let them cross over into another country every day of the school year because hopefully, life is better there, at least for a few hours. Mothers who worry about the horrific things their children are seeing.

Same as I would.

The kidnappings. The evil of fathers who are among the most influential drug lords in Mexico. The hooded Mexican police with machine guns—seen the minute the children cross the bridge back into Mexico—police who can actually provide very little real protection. These are the stories of Mexican children.

And then there was this whisper of a story—of the little boy I read to who'd witnessed the decapitation of his uncle. I didn't want to believe it.

He has a mother who couldn't shield him from it—though I know she tried.

By comparison, my world is pretty. The reality of border life shocked me. As much as it could, the terror of it came close for those days.

After lunch, a custodian named Tony told me where I could sit and look out over Mexico. It was a bluff in the middle of town just around the corner from City Hall. It was situated maybe a thousand feet from the bridge. I sat there on that lovely spring day, trying to imagine life on the other side.

My seat was a boulder overlooking the Rio Grande, and on a path maybe thirty feet below me, I soon saw about fifteen Mexicans, including a small child, walking quietly and quickly as they looked over their shoulders. Some were on cell phones. Most disappeared into the brush, but a young pregnant woman was hurriedly escorted by two men up the hill and into a car that seemed to come out of nowhere, screeching to a stop just behind me. My heart pounded at the nearness and the desperation. Once the girl was inside, the car sped off so fast the door wasn't even closed. Almost immediately, U.S. Border Patrol agents swarmed the area. I later learned the girl was probably trying to give birth in the U.S. so her child would have citizenship.

Of course she was trying, I thought. Because a mother will do anything. How frightened the mother-girl must've been.

In my mind, I'd pictured such desperation taking place only at night, but it was daylight and in the middle of town, because babies come when they come.

I read to one last group of students that day. When they entered, I looked at them differently and deeper and kinder because of the stories I'd been told.

I was about to read them a story of Paloma the Pigeon, the story of an innocent child who dared to hope—a story that would fall on the ears of many children who'd been robbed of their own innocence. *Their eyes have seen too much,* I thought. They already knew desperation. They were born into it.

But as I began to read, I watched the emotion in their eyes. I watched their faces rise and fall with the story and I understood that desperation cannot drown out hope. It just can't. In fact, it's desperation that leads us to it.

It's why mamas sneak into the United States with a child, knowing they will likely be detained. It's why mamas will turn loose of a crying child's hand, entrusting him to a total stranger who might offer safe passage across the border—because no matter what's waiting on the other side of the river, hopefully it's way less horrific than where they are. How bad must it be?

These mothers are desperate for their babies. We are their hope. And hope is living and buoyant and afloat.

I know there are laws. I know most all of them are necessary. I know bad people are coming into our country. I know laws are for our own protection. I know it and most of the time, I believe it.

But one day, a few years ago, I read a story to a bunch of real little border children, with real names and faces and stories. In the days that have passed, one of those babies died after being caught in cross-fire on the wrong side of a big bridge. The librarian let me know.

That baby called someone mama. She is one of us, and she will grieve him until the day she dies. She wanted better for him, and she was trying hard. She was trying to save him.

I would do exactly the same. I would go to extremes. I would do anything it took to save my babies. If there wasn't time to do it the right way, I'd go ahead and do it the wrong way. If I was desperate, I know I would.

I viewed many things a certain way for most of my adult life. I've lived my life under the assumption that most things are truly black and white. They're not. I've often entered into a place or situation with my self-righteous smarts tucked inside my stylish bag, actually believing I know what is best for another person or another people group—thinking I know all the nuances of a situation I've never lived.

My old friend Darrell tells me the source of all of it is my pride. And it is, I admit. It's also my laziness—having believed whoever was speaking loudest and nearest to my ear. Sometimes, they were people close to me. Oftentimes, they were big important people with credentials and platforms. They were influencers, and for years I drank their Kool-Aid. To have believed their words and ideas without carefully checking them against my own heart was taking the easy way out. I was letting them think for me. Maybe because I was busy. Maybe because I thought they were smarter. Maybe because I thought they were altruistic. I was naïve.

Here's what I've come to see. On my journey of turning loose the things that have created so much noise and discord in my life, *my very own eyes* are seeing things for themselves again. They've become curious eyes. This turning loose of one opinion I'd settled on has freed me to begin to see situations and people without a filter someone else projected onto their story.

There are no easy answers to the hard questions. There is no simple fix for the big problems. There is no healing balm to make it all go away or to make it all okay.

But there's God. And there's love. And there's me. It's a formidable trifecta when I am willing to let go of a paradigm I can no longer reconcile.

Chapter 6

CHARLOTTE OF THE MOUNTAIN

Turning Loose of Blindness

I worry about what's happening to us as a people group.

We can order just about anything we need or want from the comfort of our couches. We push *place order* and, in a few days, our goods will be waiting for us right outside our front doors. We don't even have to go to the bank anymore—we take a picture of our deposit and, just like that, it lands in our bank account. We can move money around from one account to another by pressing a few buttons. We pay most all of our bills online. We check out books electronically. We select our groceries online and never have to leave our cars to pick them up. Of course, there is the option, in the city, to have them delivered right to our doors. Almost four million of us in America work at least part time from home—much more efficient because we don't have all the interactions to distract us.

All the convenience is nice, but it comes at a price.

We no longer experience many things as three-dimensional. The lives we share are patted down flat on the computer screen. Even the word "friend" has lost its flesh and blood. The world, discovered to be round all those years ago, is actually beginning to flatten out after all.

We are losing eye contact. And when we lose eye contact, we become blind to each other. The bank teller. The shopkeeper. The grocery store checker. The co-worker. The young mom at the playground. The librarian.

When we become blind to each other, our ability to empathize atrophies. We operate in a much more efficient manner when we keep people with different, hard-to-see lives at arm's length. The blindness doesn't happen all at once. It happens little by little, as there are more and more demands on our time. Then one day, we find our habit is to look through people without seeing them at all. In fact, we don't even realize we're doing it.

Turning loose of blindness will always require something of us. A kind word. Some cash. A commitment of time that could last for years.

I started thinking about my own blind eyes because high altitudes always give me a headache.

It's what woke me at three-thirty in the morning on a particular ski vacation in Colorado. It made me crawl out from under a warm blanket, pull my tired and aching ski body to a standing position, and feel around in the dark for my slippers. It's why I bumped my shin on the end of the bed, mumbling a string of bad words. It's what made me slowly feel my way down the hall in a quiet sleeping house to go looking for Ibuprofen.

As I sat down to finish my glass of water, right in front of me was the sprawling wide ski slope at the base of Peak 8—fully visible through the large window. The white cover of snow glowed brightly even in the dark and it was breathtaking. It was incredibly peaceful sitting there in the lonely hours of the morning. In all my years of skiing, I'd never once stayed on the mountain. Never had I imagined what it looks like while everyone sleeps.

Well, not everyone.

From up the slope, I saw a light moving slowly down the mountain toward the base. As it got closer, I began to hear it. It wasn't as much a noise as it was a hum. A gentle hum. At least that's what it sounded like with a wall between it and me. I watched the light grow larger and nearer.

Of course, I'd suspected it was a snowcat—the machine that grooms the slopes. What surprised me though, was in all my years of skiing, I never once gave a single thought to when or how those beautifully groomed slopes came to be. I never gave a thought to the person who drives that big machine up and down the mountains all night long so my family and I could take an early lift up to leave a fresh mark in the snow.

Never once thought about it. I wondered about the person driving the snowcat. *Guy or gal? Gal,* I decided, because I'm one and it was easier for me to wonder about her. I then gave her a name. *Charlotte,* I decided.

I'm an expert at wondering, so I continued.

Was it a second job, this riding the mountain? Was she a student and was nighttime the only time available to work? Did Charlotte have babies she tucked into bed before she hit the slopes? Maybe she took care of them during the day and once her husband came home, she came to work on the mountain because sometimes, one income won't do the trick. Maybe Charlotte was a single mom. If so, I wondered who she'd left her kiddos with that night. I guessed she probably did the job like the rest of us do *our* jobs—to pay the bills. Of course, there was an entirely different scenario where she was single with no kids and just enjoyed the perks of skiing for free in exchange for work on the mountain. I guessed that could as likely be it.

I wondered as I watched if she was listening to music inside that big machine. Was she a James Taylor girl like me, or was she a Metallica type? Listening to John Denver on the mountain would be way too cliché for Charlotte, I decided. Maybe Sigur Ros or Balmorhea instead—always good pondering music. Or, I wondered, maybe *that* night,

Charlotte just preferred the silence as a backdrop to her thoughts. Kind of like me.

I wondered if she had problems to work out. I sure hoped she would come up with a plan before daylight came. I wondered if she believed in God and I hoped she did. I think seeing a mountain with a belief in God the Creator is quite like seeing it while wearing 3-D glasses. It comes alive, and I wanted Charlotte to see it like that. Even if she didn't believe, I thought how every night she's on the mountain, she must at least consider the possibility.

The day before, I'd been lucky enough to catch the very last lift up a mountain. Most people had called it a day already and were perhaps already soaking in a hot tub. But me? I felt like I had the mountain to myself. My family—each of us wanting to absorb all we could of a final run down the mountain—decided to take our own favorite ways down. It was the most alone I'd ever felt on a mountain—only the sound of my skis cutting and gliding over the snow with just the trees watching. It was peace and quiet and calm.

It must be what draws Charlotte to the mountain night after night, I thought.

One thing I knew about Charlotte was she really liked herself. I knew because otherwise, she could never spend so much time alone. I have a friend who just can't seem to please herself. She's never ever alone. She makes sure of it. She surrounds herself with people and lots of "going and coming" and noise because she would rather not spend time with herself.

But that wasn't Charlotte. She liked who she was. And whatever her great purpose was in this life, I thought she must feel closest to achieving it when she's riding that mountain. The mountain was her great encourager and her most devoted confidante, I knew. There is so much power there and so much beauty. I was envious that she'd seen every possible face that mountain could take on—with feet upon feet of fresh powder and when too little snow left it bare in spots. Sometimes, when high winds would move the fresh powder to swirl like mini tornadoes, Charlotte saw it. She'd seen that strong mountain on the darkest night, under the fullest moon and under a sky full of stars. She'd seen it still and quiet—absent the thousands of skiers in their colorful ski garb and silly hats.

Charlotte is an exceptionally lucky girl, for she has found a true friend in the mountain.

Well, that's what I thought anyway. It's what happens when I get to wondering.

But they are not without meaning or purpose—these thoughts of mine. And all that mountain wondering made me think about the many people working night shifts. They work to be ready to serve people like me—the ones who don't see them. The ones who get to sleep at night. Some of these night workers bake. Some drive buses and trains and planes. Some clean toilets. Some stay awake, just in case we get sick and need some help. Some drive the streets to take care of any trouble that might arise. Some keep the coffee fresh and hot.

And some, like my Charlotte, drive the machines that climb up the mountains to make the snow pretty and smooth and safe.

I'm thankful for her, and for all the others who stay awake while I sleep. Though I couldn't tell *her*, I could make a decision to see *other* people. Not just the pretty ones with big stories, but also the average ones with ordinary stories.

I have an old-school flashcard I keep pinned to the board above my desk. It says, *See something.* It's my reminder to wake up—to make eye contact. It reminds me to turn loose of the kind of blindness that comes from busyness and self-absorption. It reminds me, once again, when I turn loose of my bent toward blindness, I find loveliness somewhere I never thought to look before. It's true. After all, it's how I met Charlotte.

Chapter 7

THE INVISIBLE LINE

Turning Loose of Youthfulness

It's happened twice now—once in Jackson, Wyoming and again in Fredericksburg, Texas. A very handsome man dressed to the nines approached me on the sidewalk. He lured me in with a dazzling smile and a seductive accent. I hoped for a tasting of champagne but turned out I was a mission project. Both men were on a mission to give me more confidence by applying some secret serum beneath my eyes to magically erase the years of wear and tear. A mere one grand, it would cost me.

No thanks, I told them each time. *I like how I look. It took me years to look this good.*

And I meant it. Kind of.

I've never felt it more challenging to prove my worth than in these years of middle age. The pressure is internal and external, and it has a healthy appetite. My glow is fading, and don't even try to tell me it isn't.

When I'm with those younger than me, my punch lines fall flat these days. The harder I try, the flatter they fall. Oh, I see the pathetic looks—don't think I don't. And current events? Why do there have to be so many of them? Comedy? I used to be a master at it, but I'm slipping. In my head, it makes perfect sense, but no one gets it. I'm just south of sixty and sometimes I wear ripped jeans. Too much? Too desperate? Even I don't know. Using emojis on social media is full of landmines. First of all, I'm uncertain of some of their meanings. Secondly, they're tiny, and the risk of sending a smiley face when I intend to send a sad face has proven disastrous.

So yes. Youthfulness has mostly slipped away from me. There are days when I cling hard to bits and pieces of it, but I feel my grip loosening on those, too. Here's what I'm thinking. It might be time to just turn loose altogether. I'm tired. It's been a good run.

And some parts of this new place are starting to feel like home.

My husband and I were out for dinner and a movie a few weeks ago in a neighboring town when we ran into a younger couple we knew. We asked what they were doing, and they told us they were there for their son's baseball tournament.

"What about y'all?" they asked. "What are *you* doing tonight?"

And without missing a beat, my husband answered, "Whatever we *want!*"

Whatever we want. That's it! That's what we're doing most of the time now. And it is pretty glorious; I'm not going to lie.

Here's the thing. We've surrounded ourselves with like-minded and like-aged friends who are also doing whatever *they* want. Many times, we do it together. We laugh at each other's jokes. We find each other hysterical. We get each other. Some of us wear ripped jeans and the ones who don't, don't care if we do. Most of us find few current events even worth discussing, so we discuss them briefly and go right back to laughing.

We hike and we bike. We apply Biofreeze and then we go ski. We travel and we read. We take a couple of Advils and we grandparent like the bosses we are. We watch our Apple TV because, yes, we know what one is. We eat good food, and a few sweets, and drink lots of coffee and a little wine for a healthy heart.

We hold Art Nights where we critique and analyze a particularly weird painting, and trust me when I say you would be hard-pressed to find better entertainment! We gather round each other when life gets hard. We buoy each other up by throwing pre-bypass parties that end in prayers and hugs.

Even as my right hand is slipping away from youthfulness, my left hand is taking hold of something new and wonderful. It's good. I'm happy. I think.

The getting here was a rocky road though, laden with landmines and hot flashes at every turn.

When I was forty-four, my husband and I traveled to the city to take our oldest son to dinner for his birthday. By the time we reached the restaurant, our dinner party had grown to include about ten of his friends. Todd and I took our seats at the end of the large table. The conversation was delightful, as we heard hysterically funny stories about college life. We laughed. We smiled. We ate.

Then I made the mistake.

I commented on something someone at the other end of the table said, and I waited for them to be thoroughly amused at my comment because I'm funny, you see.

I waited some more. Okay. It was getting awkward.

Not a single one of them, including my son, would make eye contact. Something was amiss. I looked questioningly at my husband, who just shrugged. At first, I thought maybe the cheese from my enchilada might be dangling from my chin, but Todd nonverbally confirmed *that* wasn't it. Eventually, a sensitive girl made some sense of it and she announced her findings to the others. I'd heard something wrong, she deduced, therefore rendering my really funny comment meaningless when inserted randomly into a conversation I *thought* they were having. Which they weren't. Did you get all that? Neither did they.

There was a little stifled laughter at my expense and an exchange of pathetic glances.

Isn't it sad about Adam's mom? That's what those glances were saying.

And that's when I knew it. I knew I was crossing over the invisible line separating young from old. Time to take my place at the head of the table for one purpose only—to pick up the tab. Otherwise, best to zip it.

In the years following that little incident, I've taken a slow little stroll across that invisible line, occasionally digging in my heels in an attempt to cling to just a shred of my former youthful glory, all the while trying to maintain a level of decorum and gracefulness as I cross over. God has been gentle with me. My children, not so much! Don't think I don't see the looks that pass between them as they help me convert from a PC to a Mac. I've noted it in their impatience with me as I wrapped my head around the newest iPhone. I know they mocked me for buying the plus size model. I heard them upstairs whispering when I called up, asking for help with it all.

"It's *your* turn to help her," my son said.

I was fragile as I crossed the invisible line. Was it too much to ask for a little kindness, being I gave them life and all?

In those years, I taught music to preschoolers, and on an almost daily basis, I interacted with their young moms. They were all so cute and sweet, with pretty skin and pretty names like Veronica and Valerie. Sometimes, they were pregnant, and as all expectant moms do, they often discussed it. My temptation to join in the discussion was huge. HUGE, I tell you. I mean, I've been pregnant too, right?

I know, I thought as they talked about their sleepless nights. *Uh-huh,* I'd agree as they talked about leg cramps and calcium deficiency.

Would you look at me over here—just being one of the girls?

And just before I mentioned a particularly funny tale about my epidural, out of nowhere and in the nick of time, a still small voice reminded me of these things.

Babies sleep on their backs now, not on their tummies. Mister Rogers is out, *Paw Patrol* is in. Labor and delivery happen in the same room now. *How efficient.* Phrases like *it's a girl* or *it's a boy* are no longer a thing because the parents have known the sex of the child for months. Because sonograms are a thing—sonograms in 3-D. Does the doctor provide the 3-D glasses, or do they cost extra? It's all I want to know. And are popcorn and a drink included in the ticket price?

In my mind, I snort because I think I'm funny, and I come close to asking the questions out loud, until, in the back of my mind, I hear my daughter saying, "Mom, no!"

What is wrong with these people? Moving on.

I have a particular gift for speaking in accents. I do a killer British Cockney, not a bad Aussie, a South American accent of some sort, an Indian (from India) accent, and a lovely Southern drawl. My favorite accent of all, though, is my New Yorker.

When my children were little, they were so amused! I was medium cool then. I would have them repeat lines back to me with an accent. Oh, we were all so funny—just a bunch of hysterical people. Eventually, when their little friends would come over, I would entertain them, too. We had a grand time, until one day my accents and I were no longer funny. Boom. Just like that. I didn't understand. If anything, my game had only gotten stronger, but my kids eventually thought I was just a weirdo. Though they asked me to stop, their friends would still request my performances. Of course, I did not disappoint. I was Streisand, Rosie Perez, and Kate Winslet. Ask and you shall receive.

Then all of a sudden, there was a bear market on funny over there on the side where youthfulness lives. No thank you very much.

I have since packed up my accents and crossed the invisible line with a suitcase full of them. Why just this morning, my friend Nat and I hung up the phone with these words.

Good boi. Ya nails ah like buttah.

Every single time Harriet and I get together, we become South American sisters at some point in the conversation. It's just what we do and if you don't understand it, I can't explain it to you.

Here's what I do know. All of the aforementioned comics have stepped over the line with me into a new space where we are funny as all get out. Everyone thinks so—or at the very least, they appreciate the fact that we find *ourselves* funny. Whatever. It's all good. We are free to be whomever we want over here. And you know what?

It's enough.

Did you hear that, cool kids? We thought it would be lonely here on the north side of the invisible line, but not so. There are others here! And we're having a rip-roaring good time.

One of my sweet friends told me there are moments in these middle years when she and her husband look at each other, kind of shrug, and say, "Well, here we are."

So, it seems, us too.

Shrug.

Can't go over it. Can't go around it. Gotta go through it. And unless we want to have our arms jerked off, we better turn loose.

Well, okay then. If we must, we must. But I'll tell you one thing. Wherever this road takes me and whenever I get the urge, I will not refrain from telling the funny epidural story in a full-on British accent. Just saying.

Chapter 8

A BOY ON A PLANE

Turning Loose of Insensitivity

I think people, in general, cry less these days. We're mostly plugged in, tuned out, and unengaged. Empathy is uncomfortable, so if we keep our head down, keep our earbuds in, and avoid eye contact, we can maneuver around it. We keep a tight grip on our sensivitives, holding them close to our chests. In so doing, we become insensitive to the people around us without even realizing what we're doing.

Sensitivity takes time, pulls us away from our current focus, and renders us emotional in a world that shows increasingly less tolerance for it—a world that sometimes seems to have gone cold.

Let me tell you who schooled me on the art of turning loose of insensitivity.

Benson.

Benson was about three years old the day we shared a plane ride. I knew his name well before the plane even lifted off.

"Benson. Zip your bag and put it under the seat."

"Why?" he asked his mama.

"Because I said so, Benson. Not so loud. We're on a plane."

"Why?" he asked again.

"Because we are. Benson, turn the tablet off."

Benson asked, "Why?"

"Because the pilot said so!"

At age fifty-five, I felt a certain kinship with Benson. We were both a little excited and antsy for our journeys. I was on the first leg of my very first European adventure, a trip my husband and I had planned for months. I wasn't exactly sure where little Benson's journey would take him, but I heard mention of *Grandma* and *Maine*. Wherever the little fella was going, I knew he was excited, given the way he enthusiastically kicked the back of my seat.

"Benson, don't kick the seat in front of you."

"Why?" he asked.

"Because it bothers people."

Benson's mom couldn't focus *all* of her attention on him though, because in her lap she held a very small baby, and in the seat next to her was another child I guessed to be around five years old.

Brave woman. Superhero, even.

When the plane finally took off, Benson's excitement never waned, nor did his small, energetic kicking legs. His older brother, however, was nervous to be so high in the air. His mom began to explain to him how she used to be scared to fly. She talked with him about basic aerodynamics—about how a plane is really just a glider. She spoke in a soft and comforting voice.

"So once I learned all that, I was never afraid to fly again," she concluded.

And because little boys believe their moms to be the smartest humans in the world, her words did the trick.

Just a seat over, Benson wasn't concerned at all about the safety of the flight. He had a window seat and he was in awe.

Kick, kick, kick.

The more excited he became, the more intense the kicks.

My husband and I grinned at each other every time we heard the sweet little boy voice ask, "Why?" remembering our own familiarity with the word. With all of our babies grown and gone, we were enjoying the energy playing out behind us. There were conversations between the two brothers about how superheroes would fly the plane. There were a few arguments over whose turn it was to use the tablet.

I'd brought along with me the Harper Lee biography, but I gladly closed it and packed it away because the story going on behind me had me hooked. That, and I was getting a little airsick trying to read while my seat was being pummeled!

"Benson. Stop. Put it away. Don't." Firm words spoken calmly.

At some point in the four-hour flight from Texas to New Jersey, the voices from the row behind me grew quiet as all the little ones slept.

I was happy for their mom. If anyone deserved a break, she did.

I took out my phone, clicked on my "notes" app, and began to type the bits of conversation I'd heard from the row behind. I thought I might later write a lighthearted blog about that funny little boy and the ride we'd shared.

Before we knew it, Manhattan came into view out our windows— Benson's and mine. The row behind me began to stir and the flight attendant announced we were beginning our descent. Benson began talking excitedly and loudly. I waited for his mom's response, and it came.

"Benson, not so loud. We're still on the plane," she reminded.

"Why?" he asked.

"Because we are," she answered, patient as ever.

And then there was the one other announcement.

The passengers were told there was a fallen soldier on the plane. We were requested to remain seated when the plane landed until the family made their way off the plane.

That's when Benson said this.

"Are we gonna see Daddy at the hospital?"

His mommy, the brave one traveling alone with three small children, responded.

"No. Remember, Daddy's not alive anymore. We're taking him home"

In that second, my heart fell all to pieces for this young mother—so calm and patient in the midst of unimaginable sorrow. Incomprehensible grief. I had only a glimpse of her face when I sat down in front of her, yet I'd listened to her voice for several hours, and it was only peace and comfort—not a single crack to hint at the pain below the surface.

God. The only thought I could think. *Dear God.*

Then there was Benson's voice—so full of life, matter-of-fact, and curious.

"Where is Daddy?" he asked.

"He's under the plane," his mom answered.

"Did we run over him?" he asked.

"No. We didn't run over him. He's inside the plane, just under where we're sitting," she said, giving her small son's logic some room to work things out in a way he could understand.

And then we were on the ground. There was a flurry of movement in the seats behind us—a gathering up of gadgets and backpacks and diaper bags.

The plane fell completely silent as the little family emerged from their row behind us—the very last row on the completely full plane. I wondered why they weren't given better seats.

They spilled into the narrow aisle—the oldest child, then the mom and the baby. And then little Benson, wearing his backpack like a big boy, pulling up the rear and following closely behind his mommy—the brave woman I mentioned earlier when I didn't know the half of it. Before, when I'd held my sensitivity far away from the people around me.

I looked at that little boy, so full of life and a million questions. I felt such sadness his dad wouldn't be there to answer any of them.

Slowly, they made their way to the front of the plane, followed by the sorrowful eyes of every passenger watching. And then they were gone.

I continued on my journey, and Benson continued on his.

I went to Europe and I guess little Benson went to Maine to lay his daddy to rest.

That day changed the way I look at strangers. It changed the way I take notice of them. I unhanded my own insensitivity that day when I realized my best day is someone else's worst day. I had forgotten it until I landed some crummy seats on the back of a plane in front of a rambunctious little boy.

I'm grateful for the reminder that life is strong and fragile, ugly and beautiful, happy and sad—all in the very same moment. I'm reminded there is no *my life* and *their life*—there is only life. *And* we all do it together.

The reminder, for me, came with a name.

Benson.

OLD GLORY

Turning Loose of Ungratefulness

It was not yet daylight on Memorial Day 2015.

I'd been wide awake for a solid hour, problem solving—the thing my mind does very well when it can't sleep. It was our first year in a new place, and I desperately wanted to fly my flag that day. Because our house is an old brownstone, it isn't an easy thing to put up a flagpole. A special drill bit is required to do the job properly. So my mind was working early to come up with another proper way to fly my flag—a symbol to which I owe much gratitude.

When I was a kid in sixth grade, my teacher was Mrs. Groom. It was 1971 and girls wore dresses to school with knee socks and (much to their mothers' horror) track shoes. We improved our reading skills through a color-coded curriculum called SRA. We had weekly spelling bees. We were kids who played Jacks at recess. We couldn't have candy in school, but with a little fake cough, we *could* have Luden's cough drops, which we consumed as if they were candy. To get the Presidential Physical Fitness Award, girls did something called the "flexed-arm hang" because apparently, they thought we were too weak to do pull-ups like the boys.

It was a huge deal to be chosen to lead the Pledge of Allegiance over the loudspeaker in the mornings, and an even greater honor to be chosen to raise the American flag before school started and lower it at the end of the day. I don't know the selection process. I only remember I felt special when I got to do it. We worked in teams of two or three. In my mind, I can picture exactly where the flagpole stood in front of my school. We were taught to carefully unfold the flag in the mornings, being mindful to never let it touch the ground. We were taught the flag shouldn't fly in the rain, so if it began to rain during the day, we would bring it down quickly. We were taught the proper way to fold the flag, and we took our job very seriously.

We were all just a bunch of carefree sixth graders whose main goal in life was to play. That's it. Mostly, we never thought about freedom at all. We never considered what it would be like not to have it because we didn't realize we had it in the first place. It's all we knew. Still, when we raised and lowered that flag, we were reverent. We understood that the American flag stood for something, though we couldn't fully grasp what that meant.

The American flag still evokes in me a feeling unlike any other I have. It's a mix of pride, safety, and patriotism. But mostly, it causes me to let go of ungratefulness and to consciously be thankful. Sometimes, a flag can move me to tears or at least cause a very large lump in my throat.

The American flag raised high as an American Olympic champion receives a medal. Soaring over bent beams, broken glass, and a huge hole in the ground where the World Trade Center fell. Raised over every single sporting event I've attended in person or watched on television, and raised as I drove through a military base at dawn. Waving all through my little town every Memorial Day and Fourth of July. All the flags—waving and singing in unison. *People! We are free! Remember?*

Mom and Dad always flew a flag, and ever since my husband and I have had a home, we've flown an American flag on days commemorating freedom and sacrifice. When my flags get old and frayed, I call the Boy Scouts, who, with great ceremony and honor burn them. It seems like a lot of fuss, maybe, but to me to do otherwise is ungratefulness. And though there are plenty of times I have to talk down my ungrateful heart when it shows its unattractive self in my life, I cannot cling to ungratefulness and remember the face of Ron Horn at the same time.

Ron was my family's friend, and he died in some humid jungle far away from his family. It was 1968 and he carried the weight of my freedom and yours on his shoulders. I know this because I recently found a letter he wrote our family just a few weeks before his death—with every word he wrote, he seemed to be our caretaker. He had no complaints about his current situation and looked ahead to coming home. He was thirty. I was eight. I only have a few recollections of him—one of him sitting on our kitchen floor, playing Jacks with us kids. I remember he spoke fluent Spanish and I remember his pretty wife, Barbara, with her black hair, perfectly fixed. She spoke with a beautiful Southern drawl.

I can't comprehend the heart of a patriot like Ron—one who didn't rant on social media where no backbone is ever required and where *actual* death is never a consequence. He's the only person I've known in my whole life who died in battle. Specifically, he died trying to save his buddies. I found a tribute written by one of his daughters, who was only a child when he died.

I forever will feel like something is missing. I am a child of war, she wrote.

But that was a long time ago when Ron died and when his daughter was left fatherless. It was a long time ago when I was a schoolgirl, running to take the flag down in the rain.

I think the distance between then and now has made us forgetful. It's made us forget about the fathers and the daughters with real names.

It's made us forget that suffering knows no borders and is blind to privilege. It has made us forget something we learned before we even started school. We've forgotten how to say thank you when someone does something nice for us. We've forgotten our flag stands for the freedom someone else earned for us. We've forgotten to be thankful for freedom because most days, we don't even remember we have it.

We get mad at our country for certain things and we take it out on our flag—free people tromping upon, burning, and trying to ban the very thing that symbolically gives us the right to do so. Ungratefulness tells the lie that we cannot march and disagree and protest and want change and still fly our flag out of gratitude. We can be grateful and want better at the same time. They are not mutually exclusive.

Ungratefulness is a wretched foe. Sometimes it embeds itself in causes and entitlements, wears a mask of righteous anger, and has an ever-offended soul. Other times, it lingers just under the surface of indifference and self-absorption. Nothing is ever enough to satisfy ungratefulness. It feeds on misunderstanding and miscommunication. Ungratefulness demands its way always, and worst of all, ungratefulness is without a heart.

Though I say I absolutely want no part of it, I've fallen prey to the *self-absorbed* kind of ungratefulness, and the *entitled* kind, too. But then comes this slap-me-back-to-reality thought, and I find myself unable to hang on to ungratefulness. The thought is this. I deserve none of what I have. *Zero of it.* I'm just not that good. Other people in other places and in other times have worked harder and sacrificed far more than anyone I know. Every success I have is a result of *what* or *who* came before. They built the bridges, paid the prices, felt the hunger pains, suffered the humiliation, rotted in prison camps, and even died so I get to have *this* portion and *this* peace and *this* opportunity and this freedom to speak. In some places, people are still suffering for such things. Some people will never know them. If I am ungrateful, I'm a badly behaved child.

I don't know why I landed in this particular place with this particular portion, but to be ungrateful for it doesn't do a single thing to help the cause of others in faraway places fighting hard battles. I believe we are doomed to fail if we attempt to help them without first being grateful that our ability to do so is a privilege someone else earned for us.

I did figure out a way to fly my flag on that Memorial Day. And I did so with gratitude for Ron and the more than one million men and women who died for me to be comfortable today. They died looking to make things better. And under that flag, I'm grateful for the same opportunity.

Forever in peace may she wave.

Chapter 10

THE AIR WILL CHANGE

Turning Loose of What's Now *for* What's Next.

I was antsy that day.

There was change in the air. No one around me noticed, but the world was barely spinning at all. As if it was holding its breath right along with me.

Today, I am this, but any moment now, I will be something else—something I've never been before. I am right smack dab in the middle of becoming. Those were the words I penned that day.

I was, in fact and for the very first time, becoming a grandmother.

As I wrote, I wasn't there yet, but with every stroke on the keyboard, I came closer to owning the title.

At that very moment and an ocean away, my boy and the one he loves more than any other human were about to have a baby. We didn't know if it was the boy kind or the girl kind. We didn't know the name. I'll tell you, though, all the mystery was building up to be a most wonderful surprise.

With that birth, my world would immediately be altered and in a state it wasn't only a second before. My tribe would grow. A sweet little one—a stranger to me—would in one fell swoop be known to me for the rest of my life. His or her name would be on the tip of my tongue daily. The sound of it, unfamiliar at first, would soon roll right off it as if I'd been saying it forever. The name would be lifted in my prayers. I would sing it in the happy birthday song. I would write it on Christmas gift tags. I wouldn't go a day without thinking it.

For this one, I would prepare a comfy bed and favorite foods when visits came. I would rejoice when first words were said and when first steps were taken. I would wipe the dust off the old books, and the stories would come to life again. There would be new stories. This little one would breathe a new energy into my life.

Family meant one thing then, but it would soon mean a new thing, because in three days, I would get on a plane that would take me to the place where this little one was. Though I didn't know exactly how it would all go down, the scenario was rife with possibilities!

My son with his own child. His miracle.

Would I smile until my face hurt? Would I cry at the sweetness of it all? When I saw my kind and gentle daughter-in-law sweetly mothering, would I be able to keep a dry eye? Would I shriek with joy so loudly that I'd startle the baby and they'd have to shush me? My heart had proven to be an unruly sort, so I just didn't know. Anything was possible. But here's what I thought:

I thought I might stand to the side taking it all in—waiting my turn for the moment I would hold this little one for the first time. Then I'd introduce myself.

Hey little one. It's me! Your grandma. But you can call me Dovie. I live just over there—just across the ocean. It seems far away, but it really isn't. Just a hop, skip, and jump on an airplane. How blessed you are to be loved by people here and there. You are my family. My people. Happy birthday. Jesus loves you. Welcome to the world.

Those are the thoughts and words that were in my heart—the words I thought I would say before I fully became who I am now.

Now that I'm Dovie.

At this writing, there are three little ones who have changed me into this version of me.

With each birth came a slight shift—a stretching of the heart muscle. Each time, all the pretty words I thought I would say flew right out the window and love had to remember them for me and speak for itself.

Of all the turning loose in my life past and present, this *particular* unhanding—*old* for *new, known* for *unknown,* and *old name* for *new name*—has proven to be the purest and sweetest of them all. A welcomed becoming. The most seamless shift from *this* to *that.* The flow into it was natural and without hesitation. It was final with no possibility of going back, and yet there wasn't one drop of fear tangled up in it. Not a single regret. A full-on embrace.

This story is my sweetest parable of turning loose of what I know today so I can run full speed into tomorrow—into the question mark of things I know nothing about.

Oh that I would greet every change and season of unhanding this way. How wonderful it would be to be unafraid of becoming a different version of me—to be standing on a precipice at full tilt and then to just let go. When I turn loose of what I know now, I feel an infusion of curious energy, pushing me into what's next. I hope it becomes my habit to go there with butterflies in my stomach and my imagination firing on all cylinders.

Exactly the way it happened when I became Dovie.

Chapter 11

THE INVITATION

Turning Loose of Prejudice

It was summertime when my three grandchildren met each other for the first time. Two of them lived in Europe and the third in the United States. I received photographs the day of the cousin meeting in Berlin—our one-year-old granddaughter meeting her cousins—one older than her and one younger.

In one photo, she was smiling and reaching out to touch the littlest one's face. In another, she was sitting on a toy donkey with the older one. She doesn't look like them at all—she's fair and blonde. Her cousins have dark hair and darker skin. Their language must sound strange to her ears, and hers to theirs. Still, their curiosity about each other seemed to override their uncertainty. They seemed to intuitively understand they were kin. The sweet photographs of their introduction made me wonder this.

If we're born with a curiosity about each other, when and why does it begin to dissipate? When is our curiosity replaced by suspicion and caution? When does prejudice enter in?

When I was in middle school, I was quite curious about the ways other people lived in the world—perhaps because my father had a subscription to *National Geographic* he shared with me. Of course, I wanted to know more and soon became pen pals with a boy in Africa. His name was Mulawala Vaghalsa. He wrote to me in broken English and I remember when he signed off on his letters, he wrote, *My pen is up, and my ink is dry.* I remember thinking his life must be magical. Our letters consisted of comparisons of our schools, our friends, and our families. His letters had many questions and I would respond as quickly as I could with answers and more questions for him. As a little girl growing up in an oilfield town in west Texas, Mulawala's letters added a layer of diversity to my world that was otherwise missing.

The best definition I've found of prejudice is this—*a preconceived opinion not based on actual experience.*

Based on this definition, and because we *all* have preconceived opinions not based on actual experience, we are *all* bent toward prejudice, it seems. It's my responsibility to look closely at myself and to intentionally move toward actual experiences that quite likely will render preconceived opinions powerless.

Though I'm still working out the why of it all for *me*, I've followed the breadcrumbs of my own prejudice back to its birthplace, and it seems always to begin with apathy or fear toward something I don't understand or have yet to experience—something that exists outside the little bubble where I feel at home. If I'm so settled in where I am—surrounding myself with people only like me—before I know, I can become suspicious, judgmental, and dismissive of those unlike me. I can become hesitant and sometimes even fearful toward those who live differently than me—who think and believe in contrast to me. I can cast a wide net over an entire people group based on the bad behavior of some individuals within that group. I've found humans are experts at casting wide nets and forming opinions this way. I believe my prejudice often starts there, so *there* is where I have to unhand it—in the first moment I feel it rooting around in me.

One day, we'll all live in peace. I believe it. It's truth to me. I've read the words and I'm expecting it. A long time ago, it was predicted one day we'll live in such a state of peace even kids will lead lions around. How crazy is that?

I wish *that* day was *this* day. I wish it for my children and grandchildren. I wish it for all of us. I know all the firstborns are going to roll their eyes when I say it, but I'm a middle kid, so you *know* I just want everyone to get along.

Every now and then though, for just a bit, everything lines up and I get a glimpse of peace perfected.

Like on one very ordinary day in Germany—on a train ride to Hamburg.

There were five of us traveling that morning on a two-hour ride from the farm to the city. My son, his wife, and their two-year-old boy. My husband and me. People boarded and people got off at every stop. Among them were new travelers with different faces than those traveling just a few years before. Different languages rolled off their tongues. They were among the estimated one million refugees who'd made their way to the country—most of them from the Middle East and Africa.

A mother and her two children took the seats directly in front of us. They spoke Arabic to each other as they settled in for the ride.

I'm thankful for the curiosity of kids. Train travel is the grandest scavenger hunt ever, and my grandson couldn't contain his inquisitive nature as he took a few tentative steps up the aisle toward the children. As he inched closer, he was silently begging the girl and boy to notice him, and they did not disappoint him.

The peace talks had begun.

The little girl was nearly eight years old, and I guessed her brother to be around five. Once our grandson was on their radar, so were we all.

The girl turned in her seat and found a captive audience in my son. When she learned he was American, she was intrigued and all the more eager to show off her English language skills, which were quite impressive. She was strong and a bit feisty, this one. Opinionated too. I was certain she never took no for an answer. Her eyes were alive with curiosity and expertise in just about every subject she talked about.

She wondered about our grandson, who looked very similar to her in color. My son explained to the girl that his wife and boy were partly African. She told us she and her family were from Syria—she said they were refugees. They were in Germany visiting her uncle, but their home was in Malta.

I wondered how far her family had traveled when they first left Syria. I wondered if they'd been on foot for much of it. I wondered if they'd been displaced for some days, or perhaps even years, before they found a home. As I wondered all these things, I noted there was zero sign of sadness or hardship on their faces. They seemed none the worse for the wear, though I couldn't imagine how they'd managed it. I don't know if I could have been that strong.

The girl continued talking to my son and my daughter-in-law and eventually to all of us. She talked about all sorts of things—silly things. She talked about school, as she tucked her hair behind her ear. She seemed completely self-assured and fearless. She was smart, seamlessly switching back and forth between two languages as she acted as the interpreter for her mother and us. It was a role she took quite seriously.

Over the seat in front of me, I had direct eye contact with her mother, who couldn't speak English. When my son asked the little boy a question, his big sister jumped in and answered for him. I watched the mother address her girl in Arabic, and I instinctively knew she was telling her daughter to let her little brother speak for himself— the same thing I would've said to my children. When our eyes met, I smiled. She rolled her eyes and shook her head—the universal substitute for the words, *Oh boy! Kids! What are you going to do with them!* Then, despite our language barrier, we laughed—each of us connected in that moment by nothing more than motherhood—she in her hijab and me in my ball cap. We were sitting close and breathing the same air, and it was enough. I'm telling you it is enough. It's all we need to be really okay with each other—to be close enough to see the parts of us that are alike.

I can't remember who exited the train first—their tribe or ours—but before it happened the little girl invited us to visit her family—to stay with them in their house in Malta. She then told her mom she'd invited us. Her mom immediately spoke something to her in Arabic, which the little girl translated to us.

"My mother wanted me to tell you it is our way. We're Syrian and it is our way to invite people. It's how we are."

I thought about those words for a long time. *It's how we are.*

It's how we all should be, isn't it? It should be the way of all of us. If we invited people unlike us to sit at the same table to share a meal, I guarantee it's where all prejudice would die.

Her words reminded me of other words. Ancient words.

When I was a stranger, you invited me in.

A sermon pouring out of the mouth of a precocious Muslim girl.

What happened on the train that afternoon was the opposite of prejudice. I formed an opinion based on actual experience, and I knew it was right. It rang true in the deepest part of me.

When I let others come near, I see we are more alike than different. I see them as my kindred. I see us standing on common ground and I've found it to be a place where no prejudice can live. It's a learning that can only happen when we come out of isolation and go scouting for sameness. It's the only way I've found to unhand prejudice that tries to live in me. We can't be afraid to move toward it and set it right.

On the train that day, there was an hour of peace perfected—ushered in by the curiosity of my two-year-old grandson who is the most magnificent blend of American, German, and Sudanese. Quite fitting, I think.

And maybe that's the answer—maybe it's how we can turn loose of prejudice the minute we feel a tug toward it. Maybe we should look to the ever curious little ones and simply do as they do.

Chapter 12

SOFT LANDINGS

Turning Loose of Busyness

I'm thinking about a carrot right now. If I didn't know what a carrot plant looks like above the ground, I might easily write it off as a weed and have no time for it. I might busily rush past it without a second glance, making my way to the darlings of the garden—the fragrant roses or the colorful zinnias. They're the extroverts. Oh what a loss it would be to look past the carrot though—to miss feeling it resist my gentle tugging until it finally breaks free through the ground. How unfortunate to miss the debut of the beautiful and bright introverted carrot because I couldn't take the time to see it.

I think about things like this now—now that I've made my peace with busyness. I used to rush around a lot, though.

I was a gal with a schedule. I ran a tight ship. You know the type.

Three-mile walk at six A.M. Coffee at seven. Quiet time at eight. Shower at nine, and we're off.

I was so proud of myself. I wore busyness like a badge of honor. I thought the busier I was, the better I was. I believed the busier I was, the smarter and more successful I was. I swore the busier I was, the more others seemed to like me and the more I liked myself. Being busy seemed noble. It somehow gave me credibility. A busy life is a good life, right?

When I was in my early fifties, hindsight revealed a disturbing truth to me.

For years, I'd just seen trees. No forest. Just a lot of trees. The details of life—the really good, juicy sweet stuff—often blurred in my periphery as I sped toward some goal that would hold none of the satisfaction the bill of goods I'd bought said it would.

I'd missed things in my life because of it—because I was terribly and extremely busy. Surely among the things I'd missed were some really important things. Maybe even some life-changing things. But I'll never know.

I can't get time back. I can't pull my life up on my computer screen, go back to the parts I missed and messed up, and edit them. But I'm not without options here. There is something I can do. I can quit it *now*. I can lay down all the scrambling around and all the tail chasing. I can do better. I can see something. I can write a better midseason of my life where busyness doesn't have a starring role. I can now understand the *thing* I'm seeing in front of me really isn't the *thing* at all. The *actual* thing is what's in between the lines and just beneath the surface and it's the grandest scavenger hunt of all. To see it, though, I had to do something about all the rushing around.

I had to turn loose of busyness.

In fact, one December morning, I made a conscious decision to do just that.

It was a busy time indeed—but for a good cause. The *good* cause trap snared me over and over again. I would fall in, compost there for a while, and emerge willing to give every moment and ounce of energy for a good cause.

So people were coming. Lots of people. To my house.

A holiday fundraiser for scholarships in my town brought on this particular incident of busy. It involved me opening my home in all its

Christmas finery to the public. My own children benefited from local scholarships, so I felt like it was my duty to give back in this way.

The days leading up to it were a blur. Did I eat? Sleep? I can't say for sure, but I do know I cleaned, and when I was finished, I cleaned some more. It was frenzy, I tell you. I was a mad woman who didn't wash her hair for four days. Nothing will cause a girl to clean with crazy, wild fervor like knowing other women will be in your home and some of them might open your closet.

Then I put up a tree—actually two of them, and something magical happened on Friday, the night before the event.

Everything was done.

Well, almost. Only the slobber stains remained, courtesy of Pearl, my 150-pound Mastiff. Some stains soared to heights of six feet on my Sherwin Williams flat *requisite grey* walls. FLAT. No washing them. Only repainting. My husband said it wasn't going to happen, so I put on blinders and forgave him.

I'm a minimalist when it comes to Christmas decorating—just touches here and there. On that Friday night, I put on all the finishing touches. Little pine cuttings with red berries in glass bottles in my windowsills and holiday chocolates in the candy jars.

Of course I was listening to my Johnny Mathis record, silly.

At ten o'clock that night, I laid my head on my pillow and at five-thirty the next morning, I woke with these thoughts:

I FORGOT TO WINDEX THAT AWFUL DRIP FROM THE WREATH THAT HANGS OVER THE MIRROR IN THE ENTRYWAY. I NEED TO ADD SOME GREENERY TO MY NAPKINS. WHERE IS THAT CANDLE I BOUGHT JUST FOR TODAY?

My eyes still weren't open and already I was thinking. Working myself up.

I was lying in bed facing the window and the eastern sky when I finally opened my eyes. I was almost too busy in my head to notice, but in the tiny space where I quit thinking for just a moment, I saw something.

The sky was ever so slowly changing. Effortlessly, it seemed. The canvas of black became slowly streaked with the faintest hint of pink and blue—just a hint of it. Like the palest colors in a baby blanket. The sky was in no rush to get to the goal—a fully lit daytime sky. It took its time becoming that—like it was relishing in the joy it offered to anyone up early enough to see it. I thought to myself how good God is to send daylight in such a way. It's not like I'd never seen a sunrise before. But I had never seen *that* one. The one made for me.

I lay there and watched it until I was so captivated by it, I quietly got out of bed and fetched my camera. Barefoot and still in my pajamas, I went out on the upstairs porch to get even closer to the sky and to the light that was softly landing on me.

I live smack dab in the center of town. From my porch, I could see the soft awakening of things—the fog hovering just over the river that runs through the middle of town. I could see the bridge with only an occasional car passing over it. As I looked at the bridge through my camera lens, I saw a star. Not a real one, but one hung in celebration of Christmas.

It seems, doesn't it, December days are for flitting about and fretting, both internally and externally? Maybe some of it is unavoidable when there are little ones around, but now I have no excuse for falling prey to it. I admit the temptation is still there to conduct myself in a manner that is driven by commercialism—letting total strangers get inside my head. That December, do you know the thing I really needed and wanted so much more than sweaters in every color from Old Navy at 30 percent off? I craved for the joy of the season to land softly on me. Over and over again. I knew it depended solely on my willingness to open my hand and turn loose of the busyness that had so ruled my Christmases past.

It's likely others saw my sky that Saturday morning, though likely not like I saw it. I think I was supposed to be looking. I think the reminder perhaps saved that December for me.

Candy bowls were filled. The tree was lit. Strangers, old friends, and family came to visit. A French girl, too. The sound of children playing Christmas songs on an old piano filled a space otherwise silent. A small town Christmas parade happened just outside my windows. A neighbor said, "Come on over anytime." A young friend danced as a sugar plum fairy. Another friend sat under the tree lights and drank hot tea with me. And at the end of it, my husband and I soaked in the quietness of the house and the fullness of the days.

I don't think letting go of busyness is something we do once and for all. I wish it was, but I don't think it is. For me though, I remain tethered in some strange way to that particular December sunrise. When life begins to get a little too busy—the kind of busy causing a grip in my gut—I remember that morning sky and my bare feet on the cold porch, and I resolve to unbusy myself again.

Chapter 13

WALKING ON LAVA

Turning Loose of the Comfort Zone

If I took some time to dig out all the small pieces of rock wedged into the deep grooves on the bottom of my hiking boots, among the treasures dug loose, I'd be certain to find lava rock. It would never have gotten stuck there in the first place if only I'd acted my age and behaved responsibly by living risk-averse in my comfort zone.

I'm currently sipping my favorite bedtime tea on a balmy January night in Texas. My home is comfortable. There's a candle burning. I'm surrounded by photographs, books, and a few family heirlooms—all of them doing their part to wrap me up in my life story like a warm embrace. Not being a television watcher, I'll soon pick up my current read, *Dear Edward,* and I'll take in a chapter or two. My husband beside me will be doing basically the same thing. Every now and then, we'll look up from our reading to share a funny comment or observation. Eventually, one of us will say, "Let's call it a night." And with a happy sigh, I'll fall into my tall, comfy bed perfectly suited for the particular brand of rest I require. We'll watch an episode of *Cheers.* There will be no place on earth I'd rather be at that exact moment. I'll put on some lip balm, my sleep mask, and soon, we'll all be deep sleep breathing in unison—my husband, my dog Pearl, and me.

Welcome to My Comfort Zone.

There's a part of me that wants to believe living in this zone is the just reward of being my age—the lot due me after running a long six-decade race. The cherry on top.

Congratulations, You. You've earned the right to sit, sip, and sleep for the rest of your life! Go forth and do it.

This is about the time I hear the sound of screeching brakes in my head and I have a brief moment of panic—the kind that makes the stomach lurch. It happens every time I feel myself slipping too deeply into The Comfort Zone—the place where heating pads, Saturday matinees, and naps live. It's the place where the tired, aching me meets up with the *fear of missing out* (FOMO) me. The two of them move the furniture out of the way and they wrestle it out. In most cases, the FOMO me wins. She's good at it—she has moved me to action for as far back as I can remember. The FOMO lived in me long before it was a famous acronym—long before it was negatively linked to social media. It's actually the *positive* thing that drives me to intentionally get up and get moving. It's the thing jolting me back to life when I want to stop.

Hear me say this. Rest is good and necessary. Some days of doing nothing are wonderful and needed. Some days, solitude is a gift. For me, though, it's tempting to string one of those days into more of them because I like The Comfort Zone. *I do.* It's the place where little is required of me. I don't need to have a conversation and I don't need to exert myself physically. It's the place of zero challenges. It's the place of *easy*. It's the place of no expectations. It's an introvert's dream of an existence.

Once, I was having dental work done. They gave me a shot of something and put earbuds in my ears. They hung the drool-sucking gadget on the side of my mouth and put a mask on my face and told me to breath normally. In a mere millisecond, every cell in me relaxed—

from the top of my head to the tips of my toes. Then everything turned bad on a dime. I panicked, pulling things off of me and out of me right and left. You know how they made it better? They gave me straight oxygen to breathe.

When The Comfort Zone threatens to swallow me up with all the feel-good things, I have the same response. I love it for a second and then I almost panic I'll get stuck there. I need oxygen.

I've thought a lot about The Comfort Zone, and what I like about it is its predictability. Outside The Comfort Zone, everything is fluid. Inside it, I stand on solid ground. I've concluded, though, The Comfort Zone was never meant to be my permanent place. It was meant to be my charging station—where I rest, refuel, and relaunch.

Imagine a game of tug of war and the sudden surge of energy that pulls the rope back at the last second to save the game. That's exactly what it feels like to me when I turn loose of my comfort zone. There's always a sudden surge of energy.

Unhanding *my* comfort zone will look different than you unhanding *yours*. To the workaholic who thrives on busyness, it might look like sitting still and engaging in quiet conversation for an entire hour—without a cell phone. To someone who is introverted, it might look like having guests over for dinner. It might look like a bike ride or a long walk to someone who loves television. It might look like giving up fast food and learning to cook for someone who likes convenience. It might look like sharing coffee with someone with a different belief system.

One time, my turning loose of The Comfort Zone looked like this:

We were having dinner with our friends Jean and Ken when the conversation turned to travel. We talked about places we'd been. We talked about hiking in bear country. We asked each other what place was at the top of our future travel lists. Surprisingly, the place was the same for all of us.

Iceland. That tiny speck of a country sitting all alone and exposed in the middle of the North Atlantic. All four of us sparked immediately as we flirted with the idea of a joint adventure. Remember the sudden surge of energy I mentioned earlier? Well, we all felt it when Iceland became a possibility. The place seemed untamed, like the Wild West. We knew only a few people who'd ever been there, and most of them were much younger than us. The more we talked about the challenge of the place, the more we were drawn into making it part of our stories. By the time we parted ways that evening, we were fired up to do some due diligence on the country. Separately, we bought travel books and began our research. Secretly, I wondered if my old trick knee would be up for the rigors of it. I just wasn't sure.

Jean called me some days later to tell me her findings.

"You know, people who travel to Iceland actually die sometimes," she said.

"Yeah, I read that too," I told her.

In case you're wondering, these are some of the ways people die in Iceland. They fall into boiling, geothermal pools. They fall into deep glacier crevices. They're carried out to sea by sneaker waves. Their vehicles are blown off the road by heavy and unpredictable winds. They die from exposure. They crash crossing single-lane bridges and driving through long and dark single-lane tunnels.

"So when are we going?" I asked Jean, my voice exuding the confidence I was willing myself to actually feel.

It wasn't a death wish pointing us to Iceland. Rather it was a life wish—a complete turning loose of The Comfort Zone. A dive into the deep end. An unhanding that caused butterflies in our stomachs from the mystery of it all.

At first, we settled on an approximate date—approximate because in the interim, there was a wedding to be hosted and a new grandchild to be birthed. We committed ourselves fully to the adventure, though, when we purchased airline tickets the minute we were six months out from takeoff.

There were other things that happened during the interim— hard things—because life is unpredictable. During those times, The

Comfort Zone seemed to have a magnetic control over me—urging me to pull back into its safety. Living outside The Comfort Zone— then and now—requires a buddy to keep me accountable. Jean was that to me. When I had no bandwidth to make a single plan and when Iceland was the furthest thing from my mind—the unlikeliest place I could imagine myself going—she planned. She kept sending me new information—she kept dangling the carrot in front of me and I kept moving forward following it until one beautiful day in August, four pairs of Texas feet stepped off an airplane and onto the huge rock of lava that is Iceland.

The land of fire and ice.

We were sleep deprived, but we walked the city of Reykjavik with the energy of a bunch of youngsters. We ate seafood near the docks and drank beers while listening to American 1980s music. When it was finally time to sleep that first night, not one of us wished to be anywhere other than exactly where we were—though we had no clue of the ways we would be stretched in the days ahead.

For two whole weeks, the four of us powered through drizzle and cold temperatures, with a couple of days of sunshine mixed in. We'd made a pact beforehand that wet, cold weather would not stop us from seeing the country, and it didn't. Not once. We quickly became comfortable in our new, thicker skin. We climbed up cliffs overlooking the freezing cold North Atlantic, where the arctic winds could easily have blown us off if we ventured too close to the edge. We walked through lava fields covered in green moss. We hiked to waterfalls hidden in the middle of mountains—sometimes using ropes to pull ourselves up slippery rocks in the steepest parts. We crossed streams and rushing rivers via boulders and fallen trees. We slept on miniscule beds in the tiniest houses where personal space was non-existent. Our friendship deepened.

At the one-week mark, every morning, my body awakened aching in new places, and I could feel a hint of tiredness hanging out in the periphery. I hoped I could outrun it. I found new energy, though, in imagining things not yet seen—things I didn't want to miss. Every morning, we'd pull on warm layers and rain gear to hike behind waterfalls. One day, we floated on a serene glacier lake in a small boat; I scooped a piece of ancient ice out of the water and held it in my hands. We walked in the rain on a black lava beach where we were warned that a sneaker wave might carry us out to sea if we got too close or turned our backs. We traveled to Vik, a remote seafront village where townspeople live expecting the Katla volcano to erupt at any time. We stood in front of a local church—the highest point in town where people will go when it finally erupts.

We made new friends.

Siggy was a dentist who owned several tiny guest cottages in the northern town of Husavik. We stayed in one of them. A local EMT named Runar brought us ground lamb one night so Ken could grill the most delicious lamb burgers. When we told Siggy we had so many questions about Iceland, he said, "Make a list and I'll answer them all." And he did, as he served us wine, dried fish, smoked trout, and licorice around his table.

We met Lena, Alejandro, and Jan on a whale-watching expedition where a few of us were hunkered down at the back of the boat, willing ourselves not to retch. When we randomly crossed paths again a few days later, we felt like we'd found long-lost comrades. They joined us in our tiny house for wine, cheese, and stories. They were young, energetic, and opinionated. Even though they were the ages of our own children, we became fast friends over one common thing—our great Icelandic adventure, where each of us unhanded our personal comfort zones in a million little and big ways.

On our last day in Iceland, we found a treasure trove of colorful sea glass on a black lava beach near Stokkseyri. The pieces of glass live in a bowl on my coffee table and are the truest reminder of the treasure that lives just on the other side of The Comfort Zone. To find it, I need only to open my hand and turn loose.

Listen to me. Gravity is real. It wants nothing more than to pull me down into a comfy chair and hold me there. It offers me a blanket for snuggling and a warm cup of cocoa. It is so very enticing, and with the passing of each year of my life, it becomes more and more challenging to defy gravity and to keep moving. However, every time we rise up with great intention to head to fluid places and uncertain waters, we kick gravity in the tail. When we forgo *playing it safe* in favor of simply *playing*, we unhand The Comfort Zone.

Imagine two middle-aged gals crossing a rushing river by way of a felled tree. One yells back to the other, "Hey, what do you think our kids would say if they knew we were doing this?" They laugh and then the other one shouts an answer that can be heard over the roar of the water.

"They can never find out!"

Sometimes when I unhand my comfort zone, I find myself in the neighboring town at a new restaurant trying something called *pho*. And sometimes, in the most thrilling turn of events, I get to walk on lava.

Chapter 14

WE WOULD BE FRIENDS

Turning Loose of Differences

Our differences might very well be our demise.

I'm completely certain it was never intended to be like this—this demonizing of differences that gives me a constant ache in my belly. When I think things have reached a tipping point and I can do nothing—when it seems an unattainable feat to take on world differences—I am reminded *whole-world* differences are simply an accumulation of a lot of *regular-people* differences—my differences. *Your* differences. Honestly, I am bone-weary from seeing your differences as deficits, and I am just about ready to pass out from defending mine to you.

We are all layered people.

Layered, complex, and beautifully afflicted people.

We weren't born that way, though—with all the layers. We were born naked and innocent and the closest to God's image as we would ever be in our lives.

Almost immediately though, the layering began. We took on the name of *daughter* or *son*. We had ethnicity. We had a place in a family—a certain position in the pecking order. Some of us had a typical family, but others of us had an atypical one. Actually, the line between the two is blurred because atypical can seem typical when it's all we know.

Some of us were born into a life of the sweetest affection and some of us weren't. Sometimes we were abandoned and sometimes we were found again. Sometimes we were lost forever. Sometimes we were mistreated, neglected, and ignored. Sometimes we were the golden child and sometimes we couldn't do anything right. Sometimes we had friends, or we didn't. We had acne or we had clear skin. Sometimes we were bullied because we were chubby. Or we were bulimic. We had boyfriends and girlfriends, or we didn't. We got embarrassed. We got humiliated. We got in trouble and sometimes, we got rewarded. We were homecoming queens, athletes, and band kids. Some of us were nerds. We drank alcohol or we didn't. We did drugs or we didn't. We slept around or we didn't. We all got a reputation of some sort. We were *goody two-shoes* or we were *the bad kid* or just the kid in the middle of two extremes.

Without even knowing it was happening, we accumulated layer after layer of good and bad stuff which we wore into the world. We grew and we layered as if we were preparing for some unforeseen cold.

We graduated high school or not. We went to college or we didn't. We worked in a high-paying job, a decent job, or a minimum wage one. Or no job at all. We earned prestige with our job title or we didn't. Sometimes we were embarrassed by the job we did, but we still did it. Sometimes we made a load of cash. Sometimes we required government assistance for a bit. Sometimes we lived off government assistance for our whole life. Sometimes we worked our tails off, and sometimes, we were on the lazy side. Sometimes we were happy with our choices. Sometimes we were unhappy with our choices. And sometimes we were angry about how life turned out. Sometimes we did something about it, but sometimes we didn't know what to do about it, so we just stayed there forever. People we love died. Or left us in other ways. Some of us had success followed by failure followed by success—a repetitive cycle. Some of us wanted to be noticed. Some of us wanted to fade into the background. Some of us gave everything for others, while some of us couldn't see beyond ourselves. Some of us learned to lie and some of us never could.

Layers.

Some of us married. Some had happy marriages, and some had abusive marriages. Some had only "meh" marriages. Some eventually divorced. Some never married at all—some out of choice and some because time ran out. Some of us never had kids because we physically couldn't or because we didn't want them. But some had babies and became parents, in which case, a whole other cycle of *fully naked* to *fully layered* started again.

We are all layered people—layered with good stuff and bad stuff informing who we are and how we act. Some of our layers are lovely and colored beautifully. Others are ugly with a noticeable stench.

So we are different, you and me. We're all just who we are.

Though we may differ in *many* ways—even in most ways—in some ways, we're the same. Every man or woman shares some common thing with the next one. On some level, we are the same. *Exactly* the same. It's in *this* place—this place of likeness— where I can show you grace. If I can find even a single thing we have in common, my heart can become—at least in that space and in that instance—soft toward you.

My own journey has crossed paths with God, so I know what I am called to. I can't pretend I don't know. I'm called to love. Period. All the time. I don't have to agree, I just have to love. It can only happen by extending grace when everything in me says I'm crazy to do so.

One day, out of the blue, I came face-to-face with a man who used to be a trusted family friend. Our families shared meals together often. We helped each other with big projects, and all the while, he was deceitful and evil and a destroyer of innocence toward his own. He was sick. When his sickness came to light, I swore I would never have another interaction with him. Ever. I'd trusted my children with him, unknowingly putting them in the most horrible kind of risk. I swore I would never speak his name again. When he came back into my world and I had to pass him on the road or see him from a distance, he sickened me. In my heart, though, I knew one day I would have to deal with my disdain for him. And I did.

When the day came, it was at his workplace. I didn't see it coming. It was awkward when he suddenly appeared in front of me and asked if he could help me find something. I asked for the information I needed and tried to make a quick exit. As I turned my back to leave, I heard him speak my name.

Though I wanted to keep going and pretend I never heard him, *I couldn't do it*. I couldn't do it. So I turned toward him.

I was silent, but he spoke. He reminded me of a time fifteen years ago when I gave him some music to help him get through a rough time. It was a time when I mistakenly believed he was the victim and not the victimizer. He let me believe it then. He deceived me and my family and everyone he knew, but on that day and in that face-to-face moment, his eyes welled with tears as he told me the music continued to help him. He told me he still listened to it daily. He told me he just wanted me to know it.

He wasn't deceiving me *that* day. He knew I knew everything—the whole sordid story. His body had become broken and sick, and you know what I suddenly saw in that moment? Do you know what I did not want to see? I saw the tender layer of him that was drenched in regret, loss, and sadness. Because I am well acquainted with those things in myself, I saw him standing there—where all the other junk and differences fell to the wayside. I found "likeness" with him and I was unable to withhold even a morsel of grace from him.

"Thank you for telling me, Joe" I said. I called him by his name—the same name I swore I would never utter again. And when I turned to go, something resembling liberation stirred in my chest. It was a particular kind of peace.

Only grace would allow for that. Grace, in this case, was an unhanding of differences and all the judgment that had come with it. As with most intangible things I've turned loose, it began with an awakening—in this case, the truth that my arms weren't strong enough to hold both the weight of difference and the weight of love. I had to choose to let one of them go. With every difference I encounter, I get to choose again. I get to settle it for me. I am a part of the whole, and what I decide in the matter changes the air around me.

In these ugly times of political unrest and chaos, maybe it wouldn't hurt us to remember this—that buried inside imperfect leader wannabe people who spew poison at each other, there are some layers of them that look just like yours and mine. Humbling, isn't it?

Buried inside people who will vote for the *other side* in future elections, there is at least one layer in them that is like me. It's an important layer, because it's where I can understand them a little. Even a single moment of clarity is enough. When I see the *likeness*, I feel a momentary tenderness that overshadows the differences just a bit. With my newfound sight, I find my only choice is to show some grace—to let go of our differences.

It's enough.

Lord have mercy on us all if we forget the necessity of grace in this world—the beauty of giving away something that isn't deserved and doesn't make sense simply because we can.

I know as clear as a bell our differences were never meant to divide. They were actually intended to be our superpowers.

Chapter 15

THE ACTRESS, THE STEINWAY, AND ME

Turning Loose of Humiliation

There are days when I wake up with an extra spring in my step because something exciting is going to happen to me in the next twenty-four hours. Something new. Something I'm well prepared to take on. Something that gives me a few nervous, but healthy, butterflies in my stomach.

And then sometimes this happens:

In a mere two hours, it all goes sideways, and I want to run away, because as you might remember, I'm innately a hider. The day becomes some sort of weird time warp where I imagine it will never end and I'll keep swirling around in its misery forever. Like a toilet bowl that refuses to flush, continuing to swish the waste around and around and around for eternity. Yes. That's an adequate description of how I felt on what began as a beautiful spring day—a day where I got all tangled up in humiliation.

It came about because I was a piano teacher, not to be confused with a professional pianist. There's a distinct difference.

My daughter knows a lot of cool people, and one of them happens to be a young filmmaker. The filmmaker rang me up one day to ask if I wanted to play the piano for a movie she was working on. They needed someone to record three simple songs a lead actress would sing along with. I wouldn't be in the movie, just the audio of me playing piano as the actress would sing along. They were simple songs, she said. A couple of old Marilyn Monroe songs and a hymn. I said yes and they sent the music over.

I looked up the actress and found her to be an accomplished actress of considerable years. I know as we get older, we tend to lose the high range in our voices. The songs were in a key I thought might be too high for her. So I pulled an old rusty skill out of my bag of tricks and transposed the songs into four different keys. It took me quite a while, but I was proud of my work and felt incredibly well prepared. The day came, and off I went.

When I arrived at the location, it was a country church with the most beautiful old, upright Steinway piano. The young sound guy was setting up. I met the director who seemed really nice. My daughter's friend was working elsewhere that day. Soon, the lead actress arrived and there was a palatable shift in the room as everyone immediately became serious and kind of nervous. Once sound was set, it was time for the actress and me to get to work. To help her prepare, they'd given her the songs in advance to listen to. She sat down next to me on the piano bench and couldn't quite get the melody right. Hmm. Maybe someone didn't do their homework. Whatever the case, I could tell it was frustrating her. In an abundance of helpfulness, I began to sing along with her, since I knew the songs by heart after all my practice. She slowly turned to me and we locked eyes. With little emotion in her deep and beautiful international voice, she said, "Please stop doing that." She said it in a monotone. To *me*, the friendly gal from Texas, who only wanted to help. It kind of scared me, truth be told. She reminded me of Bette Davis in *Hush...Hush, Sweet Charlotte.* So I stopped, and my face suddenly felt hot from the reprimand.

After some time of not nailing it, it was clear she blamed me. Her heavy sighs fell on me like arrows hitting their mark. It got quiet. We could've heard a pin drop. She took a dramatic pause before announcing exactly how she would proceed from that point forward, and of course, we were the definition of accommodating. She would simply put her earbuds in and sing along with the recording as I played on piano. In theory, it was a good plan. However, the beautiful old Steinway was about a half step out of tune from the audio she was hearing in her ears. Yeah. Therefore, in order to play in tune with the temperamental, award-winning actress, I would have to transpose. Again. With an audience. Against the clock. I began to sweat profusely. We were two hours in, and basically starting over. This was not how I expected my Hollywood debut would go down. Uh-uh. Not at all. Okay, so it wasn't *exactly* a Hollywood debut, but it was the closest I'd ever get.

Just then, the director called for a lunch break. I didn't order anything because I suddenly had no confidence in my ability to swallow or keep food down. Everyone else ate their lunches on the pews in the little church. I was quietly playing and transposing the songs at the piano, when the sound guy came and whispered to me what the director had whispered to him. The actress was bothered by my playing and would rather eat in silence. I mean, how should I have felt about that? Is there any other emotion I could've felt except humiliation? So of course, I stopped playing, excusing myself to go to the bathroom located in another building. Once safely inside, the voice inside my head told me, *Make a run for it. Go ahead and do it now. You don't know any of those people, and after today, you'll never see them again. So run. Fast as you can!*

I'd never experienced such an urge to flee.

And I would've, too, had I not thought of my daughter's sweet friend who I feared would get raked over the coals for hiring me—a small-town piano teacher who was proving, minute by minute, her lack of qualification. Actually, wait a minute. I *was* qualified. But then the old Steinway glitch happened. And then the humiliation. I felt it in every pore of my skin and in that instant, I owned the label the actress gave me. Failure. I easily slipped into the role, as pleasers are bent to do. I would wear the role the rest of the day.

I slowly walked back to the little church to a tune playing in my head. It was a funeral dirge, as I walked the plank.

Back inside, I began transposing, with whispers behind me asking why it was taking so long. Did they think I couldn't hear them? It was awfully mean, I thought. My new friend, The Sound Guy, had my back though, as he explained what I was doing. Eventually, I was ready for the actress to sing along. I lost all track of time and I couldn't feel my fingers touching the keys. I just needed to finish. Oops. Made a boo-boo. Start again, and then the first song was done. Then the second. And finally, the third. A car quickly swooped in to collect the actress and she disappeared just like that. I had exhausted her, it seemed.

The sweet director was kind and requested I be on set for something they called support on the day the scene I'd played for was to be shot. She said someone would give me a call. I smiled and said thank you, but in my mind, I thought *fat chance*. I fled the forty-five miles home, glad to be done with the whole sordid affair. But the miles did nothing to assuage my humiliation. I was fifty-five years old and still able to be humiliated by others.

When I was ten years old, a boy named Tony stood in front of my fifth-grade class and announced, "Dana Knox's pants are unzipped!" They were red, white, and blue striped bell-bottoms, I remember. I thought I was so fancy in them, and Tony ruined it. I remember running to the bathroom in tears. I thought it was the greatest humiliation anyone had ever suffered, though I probably couldn't even spell humiliation. You know how I handled it? I dried it up, zipped up, and walked right back to the classroom and let it go. And it *did* go. The memory of the fifth grade me dealing with humiliation actually provided some levity to me as I drove home that day. The *kid* me instructing the *grown-up* me.

A week later, when I received the call about where and what time I should be on set, I already knew I would go. I'd planned on it. I planned to walk right back into a place where I would breathe the same air as my humiliator.

A few days later, I pulled into Willie Nelson's ranch, where his tour bus sat just inside the entrance. I drove right in like I belonged there, because I actually *did* belong there, after doing the work I was hired to do. I eventually wandered under a tent where my only movie friend, Nice Sound Guy, was working. We chatted for a bit. Then Willie walked right up in front of me, gave me a little wink and said hello as the sound guy secured a small microphone to his jacket. I smiled and said hello back, as I considered the man in front of me, wondering about all the times he'd turned loose of humiliation in his colorful career. None of it mattered. None of it had any staying power. I know it because the man is inarguably the most beloved Texan of all time.

Listen. It's so easy to hang on to humiliation—to let it ruin us for the second act. To let it send us into hiding so we won't come around to enjoy the rest of the story. I walked away from the day of the recording totally humiliated because I couldn't please one very difficult human on one certain day. It was *one* day. I've lived almost *twenty-two thousand* of them. Of course, we can probably avoid humiliation altogether if we stop putting ourselves out there—if we quit trying new things that challenge us. But where's the fun in that?

When I turned loose of my humiliation, I found myself eating at a big outdoor table with the cast and crew of a movie. It was an experience I'd never had before, and it was incredibly interesting to see how a movie comes together. The actress was busy working the whole day, so we never crossed paths. By then, I'd put the whole humiliation to bed, so it had no power to steal the intrigue of the present day. And now, the whole incident—both sour and sweet—is part of my story. My very own, microscopic brush with Hollywood, if you will. It's become a funny memory now.

The little film eventually premiered in Austin. When I finally watched it a few months ago, the morning of the anguished recording had been whittled down to about five seconds in the film. No trace of my humiliation at all. Humiliations come, and then they are mostly forgotten by everyone else by the end of the day. So I figure I might as well forget about them, too. Hold them, turn them loose, and get right back at it.

And that's a wrap. Thank goodness!

Chapter 16

BLUE CHRISTMAS

Turning Loose of Expectations

I am genetically predisposed to expect. It's hardwired in my DNA, and I come from a long line of *expectors*. And because God has a sense of humor, I guess he thought it would be fun to also make me a pleaser. An accommodator. The sprinkler of let's-all-get-along fairy dust. Here's how it's worked out so far:

The pleaser in me is the dominant gene, while the recessive *expector* in me tends to let other dominant expectors turn me into a lap dog. A lap dog with a stomachache. It is the most suffocating feeling in the world to try to meet expectations. As I am putty in the expector's hands, trying to keep them happy, rest assured I am resenting the heck out of them, plotting and planning how I will avoid their expectation traps in the future. I know what they're up to, because I am one of them. Recessively speaking.

Because of these experiences, I vowed I would never place selfish expectations on others. Not friends. Not my husband. And most certainly, not on my kids. In fact, I made my husband promise me he would put duct tape over my mouth and shove me in a closet if the *expector* in me starts to manipulate my grown kids.

So far so good, but here's the thing: Just because the *pleaser* in me is more dominant than the *expector*, it doesn't mean I don't expect. It means this: The *pleaser* in me shoves the *expector* in me way down in my insides so it doesn't show its ugly face to anyone else.

Some years ago, a friend shared with me her mantra as her kids and mine began flying the coop. It's this. *Always welcome, never expected.* I love it. I really do. But I'm not sure I mean it when I say it. You'd never know it though, because my voice sounds sweet and my face appears to be oh so understanding.

On the surface, I am pleasing away. But in my heart, I'm expecting. In my heart, my feelings get stepped on. In my heart, I pout. It's unsustainable and one day, I knew it might just blow up.

It didn't happen that way. There wasn't an explosion or a knock-down-drag-out or anything. There was, however, an entire December day when I was alone, and I allowed all of my most unrealistic expectations to come out to play. They love the holidays.

Let me step back for a second to tell you that after the children grew up and left, most December mornings looked very much the same, in a glorious way. I quickly became accustomed to the peace of them. My husband would rise a few hours before me. He'd turn up the heat, turn on the Christmas tree lights, and get the coffee going—making it nearly impossible to wake up on the wrong side of the bed. In those early hours of the morning, I thought about my Christmas dinner and how I would set my table. I dreamed about new recipes I might add to the mix and I thought about how I'd stuff the stockings.

But on that particular December day, something was off. I couldn't muster up my enthusiasm for the season at all. I couldn't do it because the joy of it was all tangled up in the expectation of it—expectations which were, one by one, evaporating into thin air.

The economy had tanked, and my husband was working extra long hours to get us back on track after The Great Humbling. Most mornings didn't start with a lingering cup of coffee under the Christmas tree and most evenings didn't end there with late-night conversations—my most favorite thing of all. In fact, that year's tree sat bare in the room that day. Earlier in the week, my husband picked it up on his way home from work, and to me it seemed like an afterthought.

When it became dark outside, I finally convinced myself it was time to decorate the tree. Todd wouldn't be home until late, so with no one there to please, I let the expectations run amuck. I put on my Johnny Mathis vinyl, made myself a cup of hot orange spice tea, and started pulling out ornaments. I felt sad and sorry for myself. I even felt kind of mad at Todd for not being there—which was completely unfair.

Nothing about the season was shaping up the way I'd hoped—in fact, most things were in limbo. I let myself wallow in it as I pulled out each ornament and hung it on the tree. There were handmade ornaments with the kids' faces and handprints on them. There was an ornament Todd and I bought years ago on a trip to Nantucket. There was an ornament that said *Now We Are Three*—commemorating the year we had our first child. I took my time placing them all on the tree and giving myself time to remember the significance of each one.

In the end, my tree was as overcrowded as always—not fancy like the trees some of my friends decorated. I never had a theme, and I was always satisfied with it. Even in my melancholy, I was satisfied. I remembered one year when my dad looked at the tree and said, "Now that's exactly what a Christmas tree should look like." It's looked the same ever since.

And that's when it hit me. If it was sameness I wanted at Christmastime, I would have to look to my tree for it because other than the reason we celebrate, from there moving forward, no two of our Christmases would ever look the same. The people who sit around my table would not look the same. My *expectation* was that they mostly would. The *truth* is they will not.

I could either stuff my expectations down where I hid them and pretend to be joyful, as pleasers often do, or I could turn loose of them. Simply by having the choice so clearly formed in front of me, the agitation of unmet expectation began to calm me like calamine lotion calms an angry rash.

The truth is this. My people are always going to come and go. They will be near sometimes and other times, they will be absent. There is nothing I can do to change it. Putting actual words to that truth matters to me. It's absolutely critical for me to do it before I can inflict the burden of expectation on the people I love most.

There are twists and turns in this life we never consider. They bring with them a trail of change that can wreck a holly, jolly Christmas if we can't let go of our expectations. Because I didn't know the future, I formed expectations that didn't take certain possibilities into consideration—my beautifully planned out expectations tied up in a tartan plaid Christmas bow.

I never expected my son and his family would live on the other side of the ocean. I never expected that another would marry a doctor who is frequently working on Christmas in another state. I never stopped to think that another would be part of a ministry that committed her to be elsewhere on Christmas Eve. I never considered any of it.

So back to that December.

I got a handle on it, and Christmas played out like this:

On Christmas Eve, Todd and I walked to church by ourselves to light candles in a sanctuary and sing "Silent Night" a cappella. Not long after we got home, two of our three kids wandered in, excited to be there. Nana brought her traditional dip over and the room felt full and enough. For the first time, all of my kids weren't there on Christmas morning, but *some* of them were. They didn't *all* sit on my couch and open their stockings, but some of them did. They didn't *all* enjoy my stuffing they love, but *some* of them did. And all was well.

ALL WAS WELL. It really and truly was, and I wasn't expecting it. It was a gift. I wasn't stuffing any expectation down and I wasn't faking joy. I was genuinely full of good cheer. All was well that year and it has been every year since. I never know who or what to expect for the holidays, but I've found that to live *expectantly* rather than *expecting* turns life into a wonderful surprise revealed a single day at a time for our whole lives.

On a solitary night some years ago, the ornaments I hung on my tree chronicled the story of my family and the immensity of years and years of blessings heaped on us. And it was so much more than I ever knew to wish for.

As in many other things in life, my children have taught me gently and well as they've walked me through the pitfalls of expectation. Mostly, I'm guessing they didn't know they were doing it. Through their independence and absences at times, they taught me to find joy in *what is*. It completely renders *what isn't* powerless. It's the freedom I find every time I let go of an expectation I've let creep in.

When my soul wishes for something to stay the same, I'll look at my Christmas tree. Other than that, all bets are off. No expectations. I find the best way to render the *expector* in me powerless is to live one hundred percent in this very moment. *This* one—without measuring it against the one that came before or making it pinky swear regarding the one to come after.

Chapter 17

EDITH'S PINK FLAMINGOS

Turning Loose of a Life of Pleasing

"Oh, the thinks you can think," exclaimed Dr. Seuss in one of my favorite children's books. It's a reminder of the endless possibilities of thought and the limitless reach of imagination.

Yet, of all the thinks I can be thinking, I spend an inordinate amount of time thinking about what other people are thinking about me. Is it just me? I'm going to invite you to jump in the parade with me, because I'm certain you will not allow me to bear this admission alone when we can all link arms and walk down Main Street in our underwear together.

Let's be honest.

We wonder. We project. We surmise. We care too much about creating an image and a life for other people to see. Sadly, we often color over the very best parts of us—the parts that are different, unusual, and a little odd. We care too much about conforming. In the game of *which one of these is not like the others,* we pray it will not be us.

It seemed a dream come true when one day, someone came up with the whole idea of social media, making it so much easier for people to see us and for us to see them. It was the perfect way for us to compare, copy, and conform. No more guesswork. Yay. We can all be alike.

We began to show each other our beautifully styled homes and dinners, where beds are always made, and our beans never boil dry and smoke up the entire house. Please, take a look at our successful children who never strike out or throw fits. Look at our lovely, curated lives falling seamlessly into place—perfectly framed in a faux candid photo, softened with the Instagram Crema filter. And the best part is we can now gauge exactly how much we're pleasing people by way of likes, comments, and cute emojis.

Please. Of all the thinks we can think, and we're thinking of this?

Yes, my dear, we are.

I couldn't know this if it wasn't true of me, also.

Holding the pleasing of others so tightly is sapping us of all that makes this world spectacular and surprising. It's causing us to be less, not more. Less creative and less unique. Less curious and less brave.

I can remember my mother saying things like, "Well, they sure broke the mold when they made her." Not anymore, Mom, not anymore. Or how about, "She's one in a million." Nope. Now it seems we're all mostly made from the same mold, and it's not a compliment to the human race.

Could I become hungry for genuine again? Could I champion odd and unusual? Could I go back to not giving a flying flip about what you think of me? Could I dig down and find the confidence I was meant to have in the truest version of me? Could I applaud different and quirky, sincerely finding a curious joy in it?

So many questions.

I am desperate to think things that have nothing to do with image, but with ideas. I'm tired of *the same.* I'm tired of looking and acting like everyone else. I'm tired of using buzzwords. I'm bored with it.

It's why I found Edith's flamingos and her double-knit pants so invigorating.

It was the kind of morning that can make a person detest Texas—humid with no hint of a breeze. I'd barely unlocked the antique shop door where I was working and dropped my purse into a chair when I was startled by a woman who walked up behind me. I jumped as she spoke loudly: "Can you tell me how old something is before it's an antique? My name's Edith, by the way."

No hello first. Just this. She didn't wait to hear my answer, instead launching right into the reason for her visit.

She said she had a bed made of "real nice wood" and an old adding machine. She wanted to know what kind of price these things would fetch. I talked with her about prices, telling her honestly, we didn't have much of a market for those kinds of things at our shop—they just weren't big sellers.

"Well then, what kinds of things do you sell here?" she asked. She was more than a little defensive about her things not being marketable.

"Edith, you should take a walk around the store and look. I bet you have a lot of stuff like this—you might be surprised at what you can sell them for," I told her.

For the next thirty minutes, she slowly wandered through the store. When she made her way back to the front of the store, she was smiling and shaking her head in amazement at the old stuff young people would pay good money for these days. She warmed up to me, though, and she wanted to talk.

My good fortune.

We talked about her old aluminum measuring cups and how her granddaughter thought she needed to replace them. We talked about her beloved costume jewelry collection. We talked about how her son wanted her to get rid of her old things and move away from her home to the town where he lives. She was thinking she probably would.

But mostly, we talked about her pink flamingos.

When I asked if she was a local, she said she was. I asked her where she lived, because in a small town, it's acceptable to do so. She told me her street's name and asked me if I knew the house with all the flamingos out front. Of course I knew it because there wasn't a chance in the world I, or anyone, could miss it.

The flamingos.

She had close to fifty of them in her front yard—many of them vintage—and she had a story about each one. She remembered where she'd purchased each of them and how much she'd paid. She knew how old they were, and she told me why each one was so special to her. Her grandchildren had given her a few of the newer, cheaper ones. "They likely picked them up at the Dollar Store," she said, smiling and telling me those were her favorites.

I asked her when she started collecting them.

She told me when water became so expensive, and then scarce during the drought, her yard died, and it made her sad to look at it. She had an idea to add a flamingo or two to give it some color. Then she added a few more and soon, people were giving her others. Before she knew it, it was out of control. She had a whole flock of flamingos.

Then she laid this gem on me: "Oh, I know some people think they're tacky, but all those flamingos make me so happy! At my age, that's what's important—be content and be happy no matter what any-one thinks."

Her eyes disappeared into her round, wrinkled face when she smiled. She then set her walking stick in the *go* position and told me goodbye. I told her how much I'd enjoyed her visit and I hoped she'd come back again.

As soon as I got off work that afternoon, I headed straight toward Edith's street because I wanted to see her yard with my new eyes—the new eyes that reminded me to turn loose of pleasing. The new eyes that lived in a head that had a brain that could think for itself, allowing me to be whatever in this world I want to be.

And you know what? Edith—who wore double-knit on a tri-ple-digit summer day—had the happiest yard on the block. She really and truly didn't care one bit whether it pleased me or anyone else.

Like it or don't like it—it's all the same to me, I imagined her saying.

Isn't it great? Doesn't it breathe new life into you?

So this is how it's done. We yank up our need to please by its hair and kick it to the curb, dusting off our hands and glad to be rid of it.

I hope I age like Edith—the Edith I met that hot day—born in 1922 and still rocking a serious mother lode of feisty. I hope to have even half her spunk when I turn ninety. I hope to follow her lead in turning loose of my need to please everyone. I hope I'll be cheeky enough to put fifty pink flamingos in my yard if that's what floats my boat, not giving two hoots about what the neighbors think.

Can we please raise a glass to different and quirky—to turning loose of the bent to please? And to Edith—who, by living authentically and truly, unknowingly reminded me to do the same.

Chapter 18

WHEN DIMINISHING IS EXPANDING

Turning Loose of the Ranch

Once, our family had the blessing of the most beautiful acres to tend. They perched just above the prettiest little river and were shaded by hundred-year-old pecan trees. We pinched ourselves often, trying to wrap our heads around the fact that we got to live there. We were city people, and our small acreage felt like a grand ranch to us.

We thought we'd plant a garden on more than one occasion, and we talked about where we'd put it. We could have a spectacular garden where we would grow enough to share with the entire county, we joked. We would grow squash, tomatoes, lettuce, and peppers. Those would likely be our favorites. But then, before we would get too far in our planning, we'd talk ourselves right out of it, admitting we knew nothing at all about gardening. Even if we overcame the steep learning curve, we couldn't imagine we'd have time to tend it. We agreed there was nothing more depressing than a dead garden, so we decided to table the discussion for the time being and concentrate on growing our family instead of growing vegetables.

Seventeen years came and went just like that, and we never did grow a garden.

I don't have acres anymore—not even one. It was hard to turn loose of them, because it felt like the forever kind of letting go. I'd envisioned my grandchildren playing on that land one day, and as I moved into town, I felt something get smaller inside me.

Instead of acres, I have an old rock building now, with a tiny courtyard in the back and a small porch off the upstairs loft. It looks out over the roof of the neighboring buildings and beyond that, over the river and the hills that surround it. And, strangely enough, now I have a garden. Go figure.

I have flowers and herbs like rosemary, basil, and peppermint. My two tomato plants yield, at most, five tomatoes a week. In case you envision the nice big juicy kind, I'll put things in perspective by confessing I grow cherry tomatoes. Yes, I harvest five cherry tomatoes a week. Sometimes, a few make it to the kitchen, but mostly, we go ahead and eat them right off the vine. Harvested and consumed on the spot—one step better than *farm to table*. My garden can't begin to feed the whole county—it can't even feed the two of us. It does, however, feed something in me a full stomach can't satisfy.

In this little garden, I'm happy. It's enough. The former thought of growing something big was overwhelming and it kept me from even trying. My little garden puts things in perspective. With so little to tend, there is no reason to rush. Deadheading and cutting back and replanting—it is all delicious joy. It takes such little time. I find myself sitting and looking at it much more than working it. My morning routine of watering takes me all of ten minutes.

A friend gave me two little lavender plants. She told me how to keep cutting them back, and I did just as instructed. They flourished. The same can't be said for other things, but slowly I'm learning exactly what things long to live in my tiny garden—things I get along with well. I'm sticking with them.

In all this planting and tending on such a minuscule scale, I see something.

When on the outside it appears that things are diminishing, they aren't—not even one little bit.

They are, in fact, expanding.

I had acres on which to grow a garden, and yet no garden grew there. The place allotted for me diminished, and it was replaced with just a smidgen of space. And there—in the expanse of less—my garden flourished.

From nothing to something.

I'm almost sixty now and I can't read a blasted thing without my readers. My vision sees less, but oh my soul sees more. Ask me to show you something that has diminished, and I will show you how it has expanded.

The children left me and expanded me at the same time—to love those they love, to know those they know, and to see the places they see. It's so much to take in, isn't it?

Though the years ahead of me are diminishing, ideas haven't left me. In fact, I have a million of them flying at me at any given moment and I see absolutely no way I'll have time to get them done in this lifetime. They come to me in my tiny garden, where all things expand. When I turned loose of my big open space, nothing diminished. In my garden, I grow some plants and herbs and vegetables, and I harvest peace like I've never known before.

Tonight, I will most likely sit on the porch with my husband for dinner when he gets home from work. He'll have a beer. I'll have a wine spritzer. There will probably be two pigeons hanging out on the high wire and two cats lounging on the steps next door. After dinner, Todd will likely take our plates inside and reappear with a couple of lite chocolate ice cream bars (lite because—as I said—we are expanding, not diminishing). We'll both eat all but the very last part, and Pearl will be expecting the last of it. We'll laugh and video her licking the sticks clean and we'll share the videos with the kids. It's Thursday, so soon, we'll hear the music kick off at the venue just across the river and it will float across on the breeze and into our tiny little garden and up to our porch—the place I landed when I unhanded the ranch—the place where *everything* began to expand.

Chapter 19

OLD PEOPLE KISSING

Turning Loose of Hurry

I'm not the person anyone would want for a detailed job. Little details wear me out. I'm impatient with them. They slow me down. I don't decorate cookies at Christmas because it takes too long, and I don't have the patience for it. When I was a girl, I remember my mother giving me a handful of icicles to hang on the Christmas tree, encouraging me to go slowly and carefully place a few at a time on each branch. Even then, as a little girl, it was too much to ask of me. I would hang a few as my mother suggested and then I would take the whole wad and hang them in one spot just to be done with it.

Little has changed.

Every year, the girls in our family get together before Christmas for a baking day. I'm usually well prepared, having already mixed my cookies, leaving only the baking to be done. But my daughter-in-law? She takes her time. When she measures all her dry ingredients into a bowl, she slowly sifts the mixture through her fingers, relishing every single detail of the process. When the dough is ready, she forms the shape of each cookie with her hands. By that time, my cookies are done and I'm sipping a cup of hot tea. Miri, however, is enjoying every smell and texture of the day. She is in no rush to cross the finish line. The hurried me is challenged as I observe her, but for someone bent to rush, slowing down can leave me chomping at the bit to get going. Hurrying always seems to have the upper hand with me, and I don't like it one bit.

Still, I like to be quick about certain things. As a rule, I don't like to dawdle. I mean, there are times to dawdle and times not to dawdle. Take running errands, for instance. Get up early and get it done. I absolutely will not make a day of it. Or at least, I wasn't planning to until the day I pulled out of my driveway behind an old truck creeping along barely faster than if it were idling.

It was a day I was forced to turn loose of hurrying because the man driving in front of me was in no hurry at all and my tailgating did nothing to move him along any faster. We were driving directly into the sun as I followed him all the way to the first stop sign, praying he would go straight as I turned left. When he applied his left turn signal, I felt my blood pressure inch up. I followed him through the turn, knowing I would likely be stuck behind him for the next two miles. I turned on some inspirational music and asked God for patience, never knowing the whole affair was shaping up to be one big, teachable moment. Turns out teachable moments aren't just for kids.

With the sun out of my eyes, I began to notice some things. The truck was a banged up, slightly rusted out older model, and the driver wasn't alone in it. There was a woman scooted over right next to him—kind of silly at their ages, I thought. Maybe their heater was broken. They seemed unaware I was riding their bumper.

We came to a second stop sign and finally the third and last stop sign before the highway, where I would zip around the slowpokes and be on my way. At the last stop sign, though, something happened that made me pause, despite my impatience to get in front of them—despite my readiness to be done with them.

They came to a full stop in front of me, turned to each other and slowly kissed. They were unaware and undeterred by the fact there was a black Dodge Durango a mere inch from their bumper.

After they recovered from the kiss, the man then looked both ways and pulled onto the highway, continuing on his way as if kissing at a stop sign was simply business as usual.

I'll admit, I was slightly embarrassed at having witnessed their private moment. The sweetness of the kiss threw me off-kilter, derailing me from the tasks I was determined to complete in record time. It made me inexplicably happy though, and I let up on the gas pedal for the rest of the way to town, temporarily letting my impatience take a rest. I was certain I'd not fallen into place behind the couple coincidentally that morning, and even more certain their kiss was something I was supposed to see.

Over the next few years, it was uncanny how many times I ended up behind the same little couple in the *same* beat-up truck. She was always sitting next to him, and at the stop sign at Highway 29, they always did the same thing.

They always kissed. Every time.

Over dinner, I reported the sightings to my family. From time to time, they too would end up behind them and would witness the kiss. Every time we mentioned it, we all smiled. That kiss was a symbol of something we found hard to articulate, but it always made us happy. We found ourselves hoping we would end up behind them.

I found an abundance of patience every time I followed them out of the neighborhood. I would instantly become unhurried. It actually became my good fortune to fall in line behind them. We'd inch up to the last stop sign before the highway and I would gladly come to a standstill for one reason only.

To wait for the kiss.

I don't remember when I quit seeing them, but some years passed. Our kids grew up and left home. My schedule probably changed a little bit. Then years later, when I'd almost completely forgotten about them and their wonderful kisses, they appeared in front of me again. Same truck. Same slow drive. I couldn't believe my good fortune!

I followed not nearly as closely as I had years before, giving them all the space and time they wanted. That day, I wasn't heading to the highway at all, but I rerouted to follow them, just to witness the sweetness of the kiss again. As we approached the stop sign at the highway, I thought, *Please let them kiss.* I don't know why their tender tradition affected me so, but it did. On that day, I needed them to kiss.

And they did, that time with a twist. The old man was wearing a cowboy hat, and in one smooth, gentlemanly gesture, he removed it for the kiss and took his time replacing it afterward—only then giving the old truck some gas to get moving again. Instead of pulling out right behind them, I sat at the stop sign longer than usual. It's when I received the lesson of the kiss fully, I think. And it was this:

Love. Joy. Peace. Patience. Kindness. Goodness. Faithfulness. Gentleness. Self-control.

All of these were there in that kiss. They had *always* been in those kisses. I'd just been in too much of a hurry to see it. That time was the last time I ever would. Though I would never learn the reason for the stop-sign kisses, I often think about the two of them, sitting close to each other in the old beat-up truck, and I still smile remembering their unhurried kisses. I guess it never really mattered to me why they kissed. It only mattered that they did. Year after year.

Waiting isn't something I do well. This kiss reminded me, maybe it should be. It reminded me to loosen my grip on hurrying—to slow down and wait for what will surely happen—wait for the little things going on all around me. The most beautiful moments in this life aren't scheduled or planned. They aren't thrown together in a hurry. They take time to steep, like a good tea. When we turn loose of hurrying, the most beautiful things in life appear right in front of us. Like a kiss after a slow roll up to a stop sign.

Chapter 20

HOLDING BREATH

Turning Loose of Fear

I remember in Technicolor the night a car pulled out in front of me on a highway in west Texas. It happened so fast, there was no time to wallow in being afraid. It was over and done before I knew it was even there. When it comes to fear, I prefer this swift kind—the kind that doesn't taunt me in the pit of my stomach for days on end.

It's noon today, and I've already unhanded fear twice. Mostly, it's fear of the unknown—fear of situations that could play out in a number of different ways—some of them not good. Of course, most of them will never happen at all and I know it. Still, I've taken time away from a beautiful sunny day to give fear the floor to speak into me. I do it more times than I want to admit.

When I was a kid, I overheard my parents talking about our sweet, old next-door neighbor and the son who was visiting her. I heard them say he'd just gotten out of prison. That night, I lay wide awake in my little twin bed next to an open window. At one point, I swore I heard leaves crunching under footsteps right outside. I had a reputation with my parents for having an overactive imagination, so I knew it would do no good to wake them up to tell them. I thought they'd be mad at me. So I just stayed still and awake in my fear.

It was the first time I remember being paralyzed by fear. And though my fear has matured, it can still be paralyzing in a different way. It can paralyze my mind, while letting my body go about its normal routine in a fog.

Yesterday, during happy thoughts about my grandson's upcoming birthday, out of the blue, I remembered when he stopped breathing at my house a little over a year ago. I remember his mother's scream; I remember my son's feet running down the stairs and I remember seeing the three of them drive off in the ambulance. Details of that night were vivid in my memory yesterday, as I was swept back to the moment with such intensity I wanted to board a plane and fly all the way across the ocean just to see with my own eyes the rise and fall of his little chest. It is irrational fear, I know, but it's the kind of fear that sometimes wakes me up in the middle of the night.

My grandson was fine that very night. We know the situation will likely not repeat itself because we know the root of it. That sweet boy was the picture of health before and has been every day since. The worst-case scenario did not happen, as is usually the case, and yet fear, even after the fact, had the power to stir me up again. In fact, there's a name for the trouble fear causes after the fact—Post-Traumatic Stress Disorder.

In my attempt to unhand fear, I've begun to pay attention to it—to study when it appears and when it leaves. First of all, I can see I am unafraid of things I choose—things that have real risks. Like riding the rapids on the Snake River or skiing down one of the Rocky Mountains. I'm not afraid to drive a car in a city or fly on an airplane across the ocean when I know darn good and well there are great whites swimming in the darkness below. When I get to choose the potentially fearful thing or not, usually I choose it. I am most afraid, it seems, of things I have no control over—things that aren't real and have no current traction in my life. The *idea* of them scares me. Typically, my fear is on behalf of someone I love. I'm afraid for *them*.

When I can't reach my daughter, who lives alone in a rough neighborhood, I'm afraid. Even though reason tells me she's out with friends and I know she has her phone on silent, I still picture her driving into her dark driveway late at night and my mind spirals out of control. Granted, her home was broken into one time, so I can rationalize my fear if I need to. The fear leaves me the minute she texts to tell me she's home. Listen, I've never been afraid to come home alone at night—not one single time—yet I'm afraid for my daughter to do so. Because I am not in control.

In this very second, I am fear-free, but it can often surface out of nowhere, like a sudden case of acid reflux. I look at the things I've feared in my life and they seem so silly. I see them as they really are— just a bunch of what-ifs. I know clearly I'm afraid of a world in which I can't plan for or control the outcome. I'm afraid of things that don't even exist. And that's just dumb.

Fear turns me into an incredible writer of fiction.

Of all the things that need letting go of in my life, fear is the hardest of them. For me, it's never one and done. No matter how many times I've dealt with it and let it go, it always seems to find its way back to me. Practice does not make perfect or permanent in this thing. I don't know why I grip it so tightly, when all I really want to do is shrug it off.

By realizing my need to unhand it, though, I'm more aware than ever of fear's hold on me. I'm aware of the power I give it. I've begun to recognize it for the thief it is and I'm able to deal with it before it wreaks too much havoc. By calling it out, I look it in the face—which is half the win of turning it loose.

So, though unhanding fear isn't one big victory for me, it is a million little ones, dealt with one at a time. It's when I am most acutely aware of my need for God, his great love for me, and his sufficiency. My turning loose of fear looks like letting God breathe for me when all I want to do is hold my breath.

Chapter 21

LIVING IN A CHEMEX WORLD

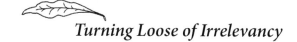

Turning Loose of Irrelevancy

It isn't aging I mind so much. I simply don't want to get old.

Aging happens to the body despite our best efforts. Short of surgical intervention, things tend to drop. Perhaps, *plummet* might be a more accurate word. I can live with that, though. For heaven's sake, I birthed three children. Surely, I can handle a little redistribution of stuff. That's all it is.

Age also brings with it a few lines from all the years of laughing, squinting, and frowning. I'm told getting a few little shots in my face can erase all these lines. Thank you very much, but no. Like I said, aging isn't a tragedy at all. It's by design.

Getting old, on the other hand, is a choice we make. We don't have to go there. We don't have to accept the title given us when we reach a certain age and receive our AARP card in the mail. We can say, "No thank you." We can buck the system. The world around us is changing rapidly and when we decide somewhere along the line it isn't worth our energy to try to understand it—we will grow old.

And I get it, as I'm running hard from it.

In my fifties, I'm no longer drawing from a bottomless well of energy. *Old* gets crabby when it's tired and is easily ticked off when it doesn't understand things. It's like being on the outside of an inside joke. It's like being at the end of a very long dinner table and just out of earshot to what is so stinking funny at the other end of the table. Now *that* will tick you off if you're old. I know because I almost got old once. Or twice.

I admit to the tendency, but when I catch myself getting old, if I pull the emergency brake and immediately eat half a bag of mini mint chocolate chips I keep tucked in the back of the freezer, then I can sometimes derail it. I take a deep breath and utter these words:

"Dear Lord, don't let me go there! Don't let me be old today."

Without fail, I'm miraculously swept up in a passion to remain relevant. It pushes me to jump right in the middle of something new. Usually with no floaties, I might add. Sink or swim, baby, because we no longer live in a *permed* world. Straight hair is the wave of the future.

When the world became digitized and technology driven, it was my choice to explore it—to investigate new places called Instagram and Twitter—podcasts and Hulu. It was my choice to let phrases like *create an event, PM me,* and *share a contact* become part of my vocabulary. I can learn it or live in a state of being distant, frustrated, confused, and alienated. Isn't it so wonderful that in the middle years, we can embrace *new*? We can go a little minimal and design a tiny house. Instead of having a lap dog, we can invite a giant dog to live with us *inside* the house. Who knew we don't always have to cook our fish *or* our green beans before eating them? We can now *eat clean* and give up Diet Coke. We can spend an afternoon learning to skydive in a wind tunnel and we can zipline across canyons. We can travel internationally if we want to because we've been saving up our points and we have two million of them.

Learning new things is the one sure way I've found to stave off getting old—to kick irrelevancy to the curb.

I admit to making a few newbie mistakes in my pursuit. No matter how careful I am to watch and learn, occasionally, I slip up. I held my chopsticks upside down when I tried sushi the first time. The waiter corrected me when he saw me struggling and brought me a pair of beginner chopsticks—"Chopsticks with training wheels," he said. People are so kind.

The first time I proudly hashtagged on Instagram, my daughter texted me to say there are no spaces between the words. I still don't get it, but I have embraced it and stand corrected—#stronghashtaggameon

My pursuit of *new* has everything to do with engaging in the world around me. I don't want it to stop speaking to me. It speaks a different language than it used to, but it's possible to become fluent. This mid-life learning curve does not come easily or naturally—I assure you it's intentional on my part, well calculated, and sometimes downright exhausting. I don't like the alternative, though. I don't want to be *old*.

The statistics about relevancy are frightening to me. I just read that if I'm no longer relevant, I might not keep my job! The article went on to make an even more profound declaration. It said that without *relevance*, I might be called—wait for it—*irrelevant*.

Just let the depth of that comment sink in. (If you want my respect, it will take you all of a millisecond. I think the same fellow who invented no spaces in hashtags wrote it. Has to be.)

Though I think name-calling is uncalled for, I do not wish to be labeled "irrelevant." Therefore, I won't be. Here I am unhanding it—here is my signature stating I will not lie down and wait for the big sleep to come.

So, speaking of new languages, I'm learning one now. It might even fall in the category of *fairly new*, but it's new to me, so what the heck.

It is the language of Chemex—the trendy way to serve pour-over coffee. Achieved by blending *astute science with fine art to deliver a rich, pure coffee you just can't live without*. That's what their brochure says anyway. I've done my research. According to Facebook and Instagram mentions, most all twenty- and thirty-somethings speak the language of Chemex. It's art to them, the brochure says. I'm not trying to be that age again, but I do like talking to twenty- and thirty-somethings. So if it's art to them, then it will be art to me too!

Yesterday, I bought a Chemex. The whole setup wasn't cheap, but still, such a small price to pay for relevancy, you know?

Before going to bed last night, I excitedly opened my new eight-cup Chemex to prepare for the next morning's brewing. It was interesting-looking, with its hourglass-shaped carafe and its wooden handle. I carefully washed and dried it before opening the box of filters—a really large box of filters. The unfolded half-moon filters. The ones that require folding.

Gals. We are emancipated! We can vote and hold office. We are educated. We have permanent press clothing now, so we don't have to iron. We're amazing. We can work, volunteer, and take care of our children, husbands, and homes all at the same time. So tell me why would anyone think we have a desire to fold our coffee filters? Is it a joke? Are they laughing behind our middle-aged backs, seeing just how far we'll go to stay relevant?

I will tell you I learned how to fold those unfolded half-moon filters in a YouTube video because I paid $6.99 for one hundred of them and they will not go to waste.

My husband doesn't understand why my quest for relevancy must impact our morning coffee. Our morning coffee is sacred.

"Do you not like our percolator? Does this other thing—this Chemex—taste better?" he asked. Though I thought it was sweet the way he defended the percolator, the silly man does not understand it has *nothing* to do with the taste.

It is simply a cycle toward unhanding irrelevancy via coffee making, and it started some time ago.

First, there was Mr. Coffee, followed by a couple of fancy Cuisinarts which quickly became passé.

That's when we began to grind our own beans.

Totally relevant at the time.

Then came Keurig and the children who judged us for contributing to the mound of plastic waste in the world. We were on the verge of becoming permanently irrelevant then and we didn't even realize it. Close call. We redeemed ourselves when they came home to find us French pressing our coffee. *So* international and charming, *we* thought *they* thought.

We cold brewed for a while.

Then we went old school with my husband's beloved electric percolator. It cost under twenty bucks, so we got points for being thrifty. My husband always rises early to get the percolator going. He says it's biblical since it is written "He-brews." He tells me this at least once a week and we've been married thirty-four years. In an unpredictable world, I take comfort in the certainty of his particular brand of humor.

Back to coffee though. All of it is how we arrived at this place—the place of Chemex. Do you know that a suggested #4 grind of the coffee is perfect for this method of brewing? Or that once you've poured a small amount of boiling water over the grounds in the half moon, now perfectly folded filter, you should wait thirty seconds to let the grounds *bloom*? Who knew? *Blooming* is of utmost importance, since it's when the most desirable coffee elements are released from the grounds.

As I got ready for bed the night after I bought my Chemex, I informed my husband just this once I must brew. I imagined how much fun I would have the next morning experimenting with this new and hip form of coffee making. I pulled back my hair to wash my face and noticed the white hair amidst the blonde right at my hairline. I shrugged it off as I applied the retinol and the extra heavy moisturizer, completing the bedtime routine with two cranberry pills for digestive tract health and a single Advil PM to ensure a good night's rest. I grabbed my computer and climbed into bed. Until I fell asleep, I tried something new I'd heard about called *binge watching*. Interesting.

Age is nothing, I thought. *Old* isn't a foregone conclusion. It didn't happen to me that day, because I was only one sleep and a first pour away from being fluent in Chemex and, therefore, relevant.

There is a forty-five-year-old woman from a country called Uzbekistan. Her name is Oksana Chusovitina. You know what she's doing these days to stay relevant and engaged? She holds the Olympic record for seven gymnastics appearances and she's shooting for more. Amazing and rare. Though in the last three or four years I'll admit my cartwheel has suffered, I still feel a kinship with Oksana. Even without knowing her, I know she is planning to age without growing old. I'm with her. My process will absolutely not involve a vault or a beam, but it will involve a Chemex and a thousand other things I know nothing about today. It's how I let go of irrelevancy.

I'm thankful the world keeps changing on me and that it still manages to pique my curiosity at every turn. It's what I'm praying for these days—to always *see something*. Big things, little things, important things, and trivial things—hysterically funny things, heart-wrenching things, and new things. When I see something and do the follow-up, I have something to talk about, something to share, and something to discuss.

One time, the *thing* was simply a really smooth cup of pour-over coffee.

Chapter 22

THE GIRL WHO WANTED TO PLAY IN THE BAND

Turning Loose of Judgment

Human tendencies are always open and running in the back of our brains. Kind of like programs hidden, but somehow still open on my computer. In both cases—brain and computer—these things in the background hide out and sit idle, ready to rise to the occasion at a moment's notice. Which can be a good thing or a bad thing.

Take judgment, for instance.

It's always there, making its tiny assessment of things—taking inventory of likes and dislikes and measuring against a certain standard. Sometimes we set the standard, and sometimes we let someone else set the standard for us. Some judgments are necessary for decision-making—like judging whether a name brand or an off-brand is best for me. It's a completely innocuous judgment. Then there are the kinds we just think of—like driving past on overgrown lawn and conjuring up the image of a lazy property owner. Though it's not a nice thing to think of, no one gets hurt because the judgment never goes beyond the mind of the person thinking it.

Sometimes, though, judgment is condemnation and it hurts someone dear and innocent. Sometimes it wreaks havoc on a person's self-worth for a long time. And sometimes the memory of our part in it causes shame for seventeen whole years before it's finally set right—before it can be fully unhanded.

Contemporary worship music took its time coming to small towns, but it eventually came to mine around 2002. The church my family attended was the first in town to begin an early morning service with worship music whose lyrics appeared on a large screen instead of in a hymnal. To a church that needed some fresh air, the service immediately resonated with a small, but devoted portion of the congregation. Soon, new faces joined in on Sunday mornings. Attendance was steady and growing.

I was the leader of the band, and by *leader*, I mean I chose the songs, ran the rehearsals, and sang harmony. The addition of this service was hard for some congregants in my church. It was the same for most all small churches, I think.

The worship band wasn't allowed to have drums in the beginning, but over time, it changed, and the volume of the music amped up. Although the second service remained traditional in all the ways, a remnant of disapproving church members attended the early service anyway, wearing their reproach right along with their Sunday best. I can still picture a woman clinching her lips and refusing to sing the words projected on the big screen, preferring a standard hymnal. I can tell you exactly where she sat every week. It takes no effort at all for me to recall the man who held his hands over his ears for much of the music. It was an interesting vantage point for me and the whole worship band—to gaze into the faces of the small but very visible naysayers week after week. Most all of those faces belonged to people I loved and called by their first names. All they knew was *their* way though—the way things *had always been*.

I tell you all this to give you a feel for the environment of a *certain* church at a *specific* time in its history. It wasn't so different from many other churches at the time. Change was hard because change is hard. Rules were rules and they mostly didn't bend—even if they no longer made sense. Rules were applied with great precision, with little tenderness to hard situations. And love? Well sometimes, rules overrode love and compassion. It's a consequence of judgment, I think. One time, I managed to get all tangled up in the middle of it.

It began because a girl wanted to join a band.

I'd known sweet, shy Jess since she was in junior high school. She went to school with my kids. I knew her family. We attended church together and sat by each other at potlucks. Her parents taught my Sunday school class. I remember the first time she sang special music in church. I was blown away. Though she was petite, the voice that come out of that child was big, bold, and beautiful. And when she sang, she was not shy. She was made for it. She'd found her thing. Everyone could see it.

In her last year of high school, life got hard for Jess. She got pregnant and married and missed her graduation. She no longer attended my church and I was uncertain if she attended church regularly at all. Soon she divorced, remarried, and had another baby. Eventually, she and her husband bought a local bar.

I remember the Sunday one of our band's guitar players invited Jess to sit in with our band. I didn't know about it until she showed up with her guitar in her hand. She was so excited to be there—to have an outlet for her music and to be part of something. Do you know what I was? The opposite of excited. Not because I didn't love her, but because I already knew there would be pushback because she was there, and I would be caught in the middle. Because rules are rules. I'd seen it before, and I knew what was coming.

We rehearsed anyway. Jess was a dream of a singer—a vocal gift to the band that day. It would be her first and last rehearsal with us.

The following week, I was called to an office and told because of Jess's position in the community as a bar owner, she wouldn't be able to play in the worship band. I was charged with the responsibility of telling her. Translated, I was asked to tell her she didn't cut the mustard—that she wasn't our type. That she was flawed.

Hindsight makes we wonder why I didn't refuse to tell her—why I didn't fight harder on her behalf. It makes me wonder why I didn't take her by the hand and walk out the door right along with her. That would have been the ultimate act of love, wouldn't it? If I could go back and do better, it's what I would do. Instead, I did this.

I delivered the judgment of others—a judgment I didn't agree with. A judgment that made me physically sick to my stomach. I was in the worst possible position a peacekeeper could be in. I couldn't make everyone happy, so I did the thing expected of me by those who made the rules. I sat down with Jess on a pew in the back of the sanctuary and I served her the judgment. The sanctuary where I sang songs and read words of hope, forgiveness, and love became the place where I showed a vulnerable young woman just how unloving and judgmental the church could be. It was, on that day, the opposite of a sanctuary for her. She blinked back tears as I apologized and told her I didn't agree with it (which seems like such a lame excuse to me now), and she extended nothing but grace to me as she left the church building feeling less than, not enough, and like a throwaway.

I went home angry to have been put in that position and ashamed I'd been party to it. But you know what? It opened my eyes. It was actually my first step toward unhanding the judgment of others. I *needed* to get mad. I *needed* to feel ashamed. It marked me. It changed me. The wrong of it wasn't wasted. In a few years' time, I would personally be taken to task by another rule maker—and that time, I did not duck. I stood my ground. I was resolute when I remembered how I'd abandoned Jess to judgment. I listened to my gut and said *no way* to the kind of judgment that hurts others. It was like throwing off an albatross that had been wrapped around my neck.

Despite what this might sound like, it is not a condemnation of the church as a whole. I love the church. I've felt loved and held up and rescued by the church over and over again in my life, but I can still disagree with the man-made part of it. This was an awakening in my soul to listen for God's voice alone—to follow *his* direction. It was actually a turning point in my faith.

Years passed. Seventeen of them to be exact.

In those years, I saw Jess casually from time to time—the kind of interaction requiring little more of me than a wave of a hand and a smile. Every single time I saw her, I remembered the judgment—there was never a time I didn't. Then one day, she called me out of the blue and asked to come to my house to tell me about a new project she was working on—a music project. A worship project.

The morning she arrived, we hugged. We made small talk for a bit, easing back into *comfortable* over a cup of coffee. It didn't take long though—it never does when hearts are in agreement, and I somehow knew ours were. As we sat on my orange sofa, Jess told me about her project—something that had been on her heart for a long time. Plans had come together, and she was excited and sure and ready to launch. We talked about other things too.

There's always an uncomfortable churning in the pit of my stomach when I know I need to say something. It's immediately followed by a long, deep breath before I utter the first string of words. I think Jess sensed what was coming.

"I'm still so, so sorry for what happened," I told her.

She, of course, knew exactly to what I was referring. It's been my experience it takes very little of a reminder for an old pain to resurface.

Jess has these big blue eyes and they were bright that morning as they welled up when I asked her to forgive me.

When I was done, she told me on that day all those years ago, the music in her died for a while. She put her guitar down and didn't play music for a long time—long years when she endured abuse upon abuse. Here's the thing. She didn't do that which God gifted her to do because she'd been judged and found lacking. Because she was young and hurt, she believed the lie of it. The judgment came at the same time as the abuse—at the time she desperately needed rescue and love from the church. Hear me in this. You and I have the power to lay waste to a person's dignity when we judge them.

Jess and I talked on and on, until we'd chased the old story away and celebrated the new one—the *now* one—where she is strong and confident and very certain of her worth.

She told me, "I've come to recognize the voice of the enemy and the lies he puts in my head—whether through someone else's voice or my own."

Jess leads worship at a church now and she has her own band outside the church walls. In fact, she's even played music on the old church stage she was once asked to step down from. When she said she'd had a nightmare about it the night before she played there, I cried, because what is spoken into us can never fully be extracted from us.

Judgment so often hides behind rules, doesn't it? We dispense the rules and dismiss the ones left floundering in the aftermath. We call it a consequence, but it's really a tragedy. Sometimes, love can't be found anywhere in the mix, and that's what became a problem for me. I couldn't absolve myself from the hurts doled out to the Jesses of the world in the name of following the rules. So, I did what I needed to do to change it in my own life.

Every single day, opportunities to judge present themselves as we live in the most judgmental of days. We take little time considering what it would actually be like to walk in another's shoes. Judging is way easier. Before I could ever turn loose of judgment, I had to admit my tendency toward it. And every day, I must keep it in check. Me. I'm the one responsible for it.

For me, it looks like this. I have to hold the thing in my hand I want to judge—the thing causing dissonance in me. Look it squarely in the eye. Weigh it. Swirl it around in my mouth like a wine snob. Remind myself there are things I don't know about it. Remind myself I am not asked to be a keeper of the rules, I'm only asked to be a giver of love. After this, I find it almost impossible to continue down judgment's path.

I was a rule keeper almost to a fault for nearly half a century. It goes along with being a pleaser. Then one day, I was asked to lay down a rule—a judgment—on a precious girl named Jess—one of the kindest people I know. And for the sake of a rule, she became the collateral damage. It broke my heart to pieces, which actually became my first step in letting go of judgment. A few days ago, I sent Jess a text to ask for her blessing to write this story. We talked about her healing, and you know what she told me?

"I received the most healing from all of it that day on your orange couch."

Me too.

If anyone (including those I admire and those I love most in all the world) speaks into my life regarding how I should feel about, react to, or judge a certain *thing*, I tell you this with every ounce of truth in me. If the *thing* doesn't ring true for me—if it makes my gut hurt, I will not go along just to keep a rule. I can't hold judgment and love at the same time. It's impossible.

I'm trying hard to always choose love.

For Jess.

Chapter 23

THE SKY ISN'T FALLING

Turning Loose of Doomsday

One day, a friend who lives inside the city limits of my town posted this on Facebook:

There's a steer on my front porch, she wrote.

So just in case you scanned right over it, here it is again.

There's a steer on my front porch.

Now that's funny stuff, I don't care who you are! In fact, the more I thought about it, the funnier it became. I pictured the steer snuggling up on the welcome mat—maybe stretching out and sunning himself. Maybe, the family cat would snuggle up, too, I imagined. I mean, it's just so good! And for a solid minute, I let myself feel completely good and even lighthearted about things.

I have to say though, generally I need no extra encouragement to look out for bad stuff. Even on the brightest, most gorgeous days with blue skies and marshmallow clouds, I can imagine bad stuff lurking in the bushes, around the corner, and a mile down the road. So when bad stuff happens, it just confirms what I suspected would come eventually. It's one of my very worst traits. True confession. In my heart, I can be a Debbie Downer. A Negative Nancy.

So for people like me, a little comic relief is like a vitamin B-12 shot when it feels like the world is freefalling into the abyss of social media, with its no holds barred comments.

But it's more than just social media.

There are travesties against humanity right outside our doors. There are diseases for which there are no cures, and natural disasters that devastate human lives. There's greed for money and power. There's hunger and there's war—war between nations. Between ethnic groups. Between denominations. Between ideologies. Between neighbors. So many wars. What's good is seen as bad. What's bad is seen as good. And then there's this. I can control exactly zero percent of it. Vertigo. The world has vertigo and turns out, it's contagious.

So, yes. It was refreshing to me that on an ordinary day, there was a steer on my friend's front porch. I know it sounds silly, but that tiny little post caused something to turn on in my brain. It was a turning point for me. I loved the way my friend's words made me feel. It was the kind of serendipity I wanted to see more of. I wondered about all the good things I'd missed while stewing over the drama of the days. It made me evaluate the thoughts taking up space in my head, because those thoughts directly impact my sense of well-being, which impacts my mood, which impacts how I relate to everyone around me.

I needed more steers on porches, I decided. I needed to tip the scale in favor of good. I did it by turning loose. The cold turkey approach worked best for me.

I gave up news watching and news listening. I still heard about things—I'm not living with my head in the sand—but I gave up all the days and days of commentary. You know, the kind where the handsome Hollywood actor tells us all how the cow ate the cabbage. Deleted him. And others. I walked away from conversations that made my gut clench. I went rogue, and I found thinking for myself to be so liberating I almost burned my bra. It was self-preservation at its best—dehydrating the fears and ideas others put in me. They'd almost sucked me dry. It burned my hide that I'd allowed messages to come into me whose intent was to confuse me about goodness—to try and sell me a bill of goods that said bad was winning.

I know better. Because cows still wander onto porches. Isn't that just the best news?

It is life-giving to cling to goodness.

When it seems the whole world is forgetting about goodness, someone has to remember it. I decided to volunteer for the job. Part of it for selfish reasons—because I found I was drowning without it—but also to remind all of us, because we're human and we forget things from time to time.

There are others out there looking for good, too.

My friend John publishes a newspaper with only good news. Seriously. *Only good news.* He's the hardest working writer I know, running all over the Texas Hill Country photographing and reporting as much good news as he can. He writes about dog parades, boat races, charity fish fries, concerts, art shows, benefits, awards given to law enforcement officers, new businesses, and so much more. He applauds any good endeavor he knows about, and he does it with his trademark smile plastered all over his face. Even if he's been going all day and it's one hundred degrees outside, John smiles. He is one of the most beloved individuals in the community with a mission to remind all of us about good.

I believe seeing goodness is the only way to always push through in a world with so much sadness, meanness, and tragedy. I can *choose* to see it. I can note its existence. I have begun to let goodness work its magic on me. I can refuse to engage in drama that sucks me dry simply by not being in the audience.

It has had a profound effect on the quality of my life.

I'm mostly not mad and afraid and offended these days. It's an exhausting load to carry anyway. When something doesn't ring true to me, it goes in one ear and out the other. I'm scouting for good most days, and it's everywhere—like at the local coffee shop where ladies sit and talk and knit for hours every Monday. It's in the woman selling wildflower bouquets at the farmers market to benefit the local community garden. It's in my dog playing in the sprinkler.

There is so much good, I've started to write it down. For many reasons—one of them being I'm at risk of backsliding. Intuitively, I know I'll need to store some up for the rest of my journey, because the reality is there are some days when it's harder to see goodness than other days. On *those* days, I'll draw on the good I've seen today. It will stabilize me. That's its job.

When my oldest son was a little boy, he loved to watch *Mister Rogers' Neighborhood*. He preferred it to *Sesame Street*, hands down. It always baffled me because *Sesame Street* had all the bells and whistles, with high-dollar production and occasional movie stars as guest hosts. Still, my son loved Mister Rogers best. He was in love with Lady Aberlin. Meow Meow, the Trolley, and King Friday mesmerized him—I think because it was a simple show full of goodness. I believe it was completely due to the good heart of the man who created it.

Mister Rogers was a fan of good stuff.

"When I was a boy and I would see scary things in the news, my mother would say to me, 'Look for the helpers. You will always find people who are helping,'" he said.

That is seeing the good stuff.

Today, a ten-year-old autistic boy gave me a black origami crane, accompanied by the sweetest note chock-full of misspelled words. Isn't that so good? God is big and he's at work here. Though I don't begin to understand how it all works, I believe good wins, though it took some turning loose in my doomsday brain for me to see it.

Every day, good wins. And some days, it even soars.

Chapter 24

THE PARABLE OF VINEGAR

Turning Loose of Hurt Feelings

For the last four mornings, I've added something new to my routine. Apple cider vinegar. It's raw and organic and *with mother*—although I admit I don't know exactly what the last part means. They say to do this for health. For inflammation. For weight loss. So I tried.

It was like drinking pickle juice before coffee. Today is day five and I quit. Already, I quit. I just cannot. I doubt it did me any good at all after only four days, but it *did* remind me of another time I swallowed a big cup of vinegar.

It wasn't *literal* vinegar then, it was words—words carrying many of the same characteristics of vinegar. It was a large portion served to me by someone older—someone I'd volunteered alongside. Someone I trusted. Someone who knew my children by name. It was a public dressing down at the local beauty shop. (Yes. In my little town, it is still called the beauty shop.) The woman came to me and I opened up my arms for a hug, but a hug wasn't what she had in mind. Her spoken words were as potent to me as if she'd thrown a big cup of vinegar in my face.

She began to tell me how I'd shirked responsibilities at church, a place we'd faithfully served together for fifteen years. The truth was I'd actually left to start a small mission with my husband in the poorest part of our town, feeling God had allowed us to become poor for a season, so we could have new eyes to see a suffering we'd been blind to for many years. We hoped not to waste our new sight. Our leaving the church was no secret. As I tried to tell the woman about the work and the plight of the people we'd met—among them children who slept on hard floors, lived with no electricity or indoor plumbing, and urinated in their yards before heading off to school—she remained unmoved and unhearing, inviting me to remove my association completely with her church. She'd made up her mind about me, and that was that.

Vinegar can look like clear, fresh water at first, but how quickly its true properties are revealed.

The human reaction to taking a sip of vinegar—especially if you aren't expecting it—is to spew it out. We get a mouthful, and it repulses us. We spew it out and want no more of it. It makes a mess, though, and we get a cloth and try to clean it up. Perhaps it's gotten on others who might have been in the line of fire, too, and then there's an even bigger mess.

Ugly words are the same, and like vinegar, they leave a repulsive aftertaste. I was so shocked and hurt, all I could do was quickly grab my bag and get the heck out of Dodge before I could form a response I might regret.

After the woman served me a cup of vinegar that day, I just could not get the taste out of my mouth. No matter how I tried to make my taste buds happy with sweet-tasting things, the memory of vinegar kept coming back—like I was taking the drink all over again—like my feelings were being hurt all over again. I was certain the woman from the shop had moved on and was living her happiest life with no thought of me at all—and just the thought of it kept on making me angry. Which was exactly the reason I needed to let go of it—something so much easier said than done.

My heart quickly became sickened against the hurt-giving woman, and for days and weeks, it spread like an infection into everything I tried to do. It kept on until I was hardened against her altogether. I was determined to hold on to those hurt feelings for my entire life, because it wasn't only a surface wound she'd inflicted—it didn't take only a glancing blow. It caused me to wonder if most people are actually just playing the roles of the faithful. It's unsettling to wonder this in my middle age because it is on the shoulders of those I thought were faithful that my own belief grew.

Vinegar can erode.

I could not get over the hurt. The things she said injured my character—something I'd been so careful to tend. It affected my heart. I became cynical toward a certain community of people—calling their authenticity into question. It made it almost impossible to show love like I needed to or to serve like I needed to. I couldn't do good work. I began to elevate myself above the woman. *I would never* was a phrase swirling around in my head in the beginning.

Here's the thing about vinegar, though. It's foul-tasting by itself, but when it's diluted just a bit, it becomes the perfect cleanser—for things and human bodies. It can remove built-up calcifications that keep things and us from doing our best work.

Then strangely one day, I was rehashing it all in my head, and the thought turned on me. *Would I ever?* I began to consider my own words and the effects they have on other people. I looked at moments I'd lived and in hindsight, I saw clearly how I'd been vinegar a few times, as well—not always with words as acidic as hers, but with actions and inactions and the tone of my voice.

When the hurt handed to me finally caused me to inventory the hurt I'd doled out, the calcification in me toward the woman began to loosen a little. The cup of vinegar that hurt me so deeply actually began to cleanse me. After some time, I began being better than before. I served better and I loved better and I spoke kinder. Most importantly, I tried to be better about letting hurt feelings go. I began to wonder what terrible thing was happening in the woman's life to make her unloving toward me.

Vinegar can poison and erode, but it would heal me if I allowed it. It was my choice.

I chose healing because I didn't like who I was when I couldn't let go of the hurt.

One day, right out of thin air, a letter of apology arrived in my mailbox. As I read the sincere words she'd written to me, my heart grew tender. Her sorrow for a situation in her life she couldn't control oozed between the lines on the page, and I hurt for her. It didn't change what happened or rewrite the history of it. It didn't take the poisonous words away, but it did let me absorb them, understand them, forgive them, and move on.

My mother told me once that I cared too much about what other people think of me. She, of course, was right. So I'm working on it—working to accept the fact it's impossible to make people like all the choices I make. It's impossible to talk people into understanding a concept they aren't ready to understand. I'm working on being okay when what people think about me isn't good when I know otherwise.

I will taste vinegar in varying doses for as long as I live—I'm fairly certain I will because we humans have problems with our mouths and our hearts. I hope every single time it comes my way, I will choose to let words of vinegar cleanse me. The only way I can truly turn loose of hurt is to forgive. Hold the hurt. Forgive the hurt. Let it go.

Chapter 25

LOCUSTS

Turning Loose of the Past

The past is a two-faced creature. She can be the loveliest friend on lonely nights—wrapping us up in a blanket of good memories. Or she can be a heartless jackal—fanning an old flame of fear into a wildfire threatening to burn down the entire house. If we let her, she'll breathe new life into past pain over and over, and we will stay curled up there because for some reason, we can't turn loose.

One day, the remedy for it became abundantly clear to me. The antidote is face-to-face total transparency with a kindred soul—a quiet, honest, and true conversation of unpacking junk. Trusting fully in someone else with our private seasons of drought. When I speak out loud—in real words, not in thoughts—about past hurts, I take away their heartbeat. It's the most amazing thing. Inside me, the climate is perfect for hurtful memories to propagate, but expelling the story of them into air stops them dead in their tracks. They're done for, over, and finished. I've found it to be true every single time I let down my guard and let someone see me.

And every single time, I'm reminded of the freedom that comes in the release.

There was a time when baseball fields were my home. When hard, sun-splintered bleachers were my couch and when a concession stand hot dog, a bag of chips, and an ice-cold Diet Coke were dinner. There was music, too—the national anthem playing over a crackling sound system, while all of the people—big and small—got quiet for a bit. There were sweaty little boys—a few of them mine—with dirt under their nails, standing on the field with their hats off and their hands over their hearts. I guarantee every single one of them was imagining the possibility of hitting a home run that night. No need for a television on game night because little kids playing baseball was the best entertainment to be had for miles.

I was a baseball mom for about four months a year for fourteen years. Despite the fact I never had a moment to myself and it was my chubbiest time in life (hot dogs, chips, and soft drinks are only too happy to take up residence on the hips for a season), it was one of the dearest seasons in my life, and I would do it all over again without so much as a second's hesitation.

I was good at being a baseball mom, and I wasn't alone. We ran in a pack. My closest friends were other baseball moms who, like me, all wished we'd bought stock in Gatorade and Clorox. We drove vehicles that had a third seat for hauling almost an entire team plus some extras, with plenty of room in the back for a load of baseball bags. We were a village, traveling en masse to games and camps and tournaments. We made spirit signs. We traded photographs. We wore team T-shirts. We calmed each other down when we got over-excited about bad calls.

Stupid umps. (JK.)

We looked after each other's kids, cheering them and reprimanding them—whichever was called for. We watched these kids change right before our eyes from stinky little boys to young men who knew the value of a good deodorant. Even the strongest and most sensible among us cried when the last season came to an end.

It's been sixteen years since the last season ended. Before you start thinking I need to let it go and move on, I'll tell you this whole thing really isn't about baseball at all.

It's about the sixteen years that came after and a certain supper at a local diner.

My husband and I spent suppertime with one of my baseball mom friends and her husband. She was one of the first to welcome my family to town all those years ago. She was one of my favorites, though in the last sixteen years, I can count on one hand the times we've seen each other. Life happened. Our kids went to different colleges, some got married, and then grandkids came along. We changed churches. Most of it was the usual, run-of-the-mill life stuff, but some of it was the unspeakable, *not*-so-usual life stuff.

I knew my friend had suffered during many of those years—life-altering events that have the power to break us. In a small town, you never suffer in private, which is the best part of living in a small town and the worst part of living in a small town. For some years, she simply disappeared from my sight.

As we sat across from each other in a busy restaurant, with our husbands sitting next to us engaged in their own sort of man-speak, my friend and I caught up with each other, somewhat awkwardly at first. It had been so long. The elephant in the room was the thing she and her family had endured. It was one long agonizing season. I could see the toll of it all in her beautiful silver hair and in the soft lines in her face. She, of course knew I knew, because her hard thing played out publicly. She didn't skirt the topic, though, addressing it head-on, like a survivor does. She looked me in the eye and spoke about truths and ugliness and goodness. About lessons learned. About perspective. About life going on. About letting things go. She was completely transparent.

I owed her the same.

And so I told a story too—a story you already know. I told her the truth about those in-between years of mine—the ones she knew nothing about. The ones that ran adjacent to hers.

Ironically, in the years she disappeared from me, I was trying to do the very same thing—trying to disappear from sight, as I prayed I could keep treading water just one more day until The Great Humbling passed.

Dear Lord. The Great Humbling just about did me in. But it didn't. And hers didn't take her out, either.

No, sir. We did not strike out. We were baseball mom strong!

And I'll be darned if I didn't feel the load of our burdens lighten right there at that table, in a restaurant packed with people. Though we'd been friends for more than twenty years, a different kind of friendship was born right then and there. It happens when there's good, honest talk. It happens when we are strong enough and trust each other enough to speak freely, without fear of *anything*—because the *anything* we were once afraid of is now in our rearview mirror and here we are—standing in the light at the end of the tunnel and feeling very much alive in the aftermath.

We are the proof in the pudding—the proof God is good even when we weren't sure he was. We are the proof that a path was cleared ahead of us, even when all we saw was jungle. We are proof God doesn't let us go, even when we doubt. Every hard thing taught us a beautiful thing and we are stronger for it. And better.

My friend and I found a *brand-new* friendship that night. On second thought, it wasn't brand-new at all. It was a *new brand* of friendship, and it had nothing to do with baseball. It had everything to do with surviving. And turning loose.

The years the locusts had eaten away had been restored to both of us in time, and we felt stronger by the minute as we told each other the story of it. The miracle and the lesson of it. In the telling of it to each other, we throat punched those nasty creatures again just for good measure.

We were the very last ones to leave the restaurant, and then we stood outside in the January cold shivering and talking more—about "super blue moons" and driving through the backroads of Wyoming.

Our guys cracked jokes with each other, the way they do, and my friend and I hugged goodbye, saying how much we'd enjoyed the evening. As I turned to leave, she reached out again—to give me a second, longer hug.

The first one, I think, was for the old days we shared. For days spent at the baseball field.

The last one, I believe, was for the new days. The new versions of us—the strong gals wearing a thicker skin, a few more wrinkles, and some serious confidence regarding all future battles. The gals who hope not to repeat history, but who know if it's required, will no doubt slay it.

Chapter 26

RINA

Turning Loose of Time

If I give away money, I can always find a way to make more of it. If I make my favorite apple cake and give the whole thing to someone else, I can go home and bake another one for me. Most things regenerate in one way or another. Except time. Once it's gone, it isn't coming back. Ever. In a way, it's therefore the costliest thing to turn loose.

When I was a little girl, I loved to play the game of jacks. There was a saying in the game where a player who had a bad throw could ask for overs—another shot at a better throw. There have been so many times in my life where I wanted to ask for *overs*—a chance to go backward and take another go at a thing or an opportunity—to take back words and use better ones the second time around. It doesn't work like that, though. We don't get overs in this life. We get this very second and it is sacred and dear and precious. Which is exactly why it's so hard to let go of—so hard to give it away. If I give you my time, I will never get it back. It isn't a renewable resource.

I've often been a hoarder of my minutes—too careful and scrutinizing of how I dole them out. Too planned in their execution. Without thought, I have proclaimed things and people as unworthy of my time because I've not been willing to unhand even a few minutes of mine to give to them.

Then, completely out of the blue on a lovely late summer day in New York City, an elderly woman named Rina locked eyes with me and for the thirty minutes that followed, time was nothing. It wasn't measured out, given limits, or hurried. I seemed to no longer own it. Rather, the unhanding of it allowed it to transfer freely from me to the woman in the strangest and most beautiful of ways.

For our thirty-sixth anniversary, my husband surprised me with a quick trip to New York to see Bette Midler's last Broadway performance of *Hello Dolly*. It was an extravagant gift for simple people like us, so we planned to not waste a minute of it. We sauntered (because sauntering is every self-respecting Texan's superpower) through Central Park and Chelsea Market, enjoying leisurely meals and rooftop nightcaps. When our precious, limited time away began running out that last evening, we found ourselves on the Upper West Side near Broadway and 71st Street at a pizza place—the most authentic way to spend the last few hours of a New York getaway.

As we took our place in the short line, I noticed an elderly woman staring at me as she waited in line just ahead of us. I smiled at her and looked away as we do and I focused my attention on choosing one of the gigantic slices of pizza in the case in front of me. I could still feel her gaze though, and when I looked up again, she was indeed still looking at me. Her eyes were beautiful and blue and knowing—it seemed she thought I was someone she knew. She wore her age so gracefully, slightly disheveled, yet still refined.

She was accompanied by a caregiver, who gently encouraged her to move along in the line. I assumed it would be the end of our sweet exchange, but it wasn't. She continued to stare at me. I could feel it and when I looked up, there she was—seemingly mesmerized by me. It was a little disconcerting and it kind of rattled me. I decided to avoid meeting her gaze again.

As my husband stood in line to wait for our pizza, I made my way to a table at the back of the tiny place, passing right by the old woman who was standing with her walker at the end of her table. I felt her eyes on me again, and because I couldn't seem to do otherwise, I looked up at her. She quietly said, "You're lovely," in little more than a whisper.

"Thank you," I whispered back.

"You're welcome," she said, the exchange being all the invitation she needed. Leaving her walker behind, she came and stood at the end of my table.

"My name is Rina," she said.

When I repeated her name with my full-on Texas accent, she coached me to try it again, rolling the "R" when I said it. I tried again and she was pleased with me. I told her my name and she repeated it several times, as if she was committing it to memory. When she started to tell me her story, I forgot it was my last night in New York. Time dissipated, giving the minutes that followed full independence to play out however they wished. There would be no plan—which totally contradicted my usual style. Nothing could be done, though, as some invisible current pulled me in anyway.

Rina was from Jerusalem mostly, but from New York, too. Her Hebrew accent was thick and beautifully aged. I told her I longed to go to Israel one day and she said I should. She said if only she had the address of her home with her, she'd give it to me so I could visit. I told her just the thought of it was so nice of her. She told me she would send me the address.

We talked about the Jewish Heritage Museum, where I'd heard *Fiddler on the Roof* was being performed in Yiddish.

"Yes!" she said. "It's on Second Street! I think I'll go tomorrow."

"This is my husband," I said, as Todd walked up with our pizza.

"Hello, Husband," she said teasingly, and my instinct told me she'd been quite a jokester in her younger years. She told us her husband was in aviation and he would be arriving in New York the following day. The mention of aviation led us to talk about a documentary we'd recently watched about the men who built the Israeli Air Force after World War II.

Rina was excited we knew about it.

"My husband was part of it," she told us.

Then, her caregiver walked over to our table, telling her it was time to eat. She hesitated—she would've preferred talking and eating with us, but her caregiver was adamant.

"Rina, I hope to see you again someday," I said. "You will," she said as she turned to go, seeming so certain of it. "Be well," she added with a grin.

And that was it. My entire knowing of Rina lasted thirty minutes, yet I couldn't get her off my mind. It seemed there were other things she wanted to tell me, and with more time, I believe she would have done just that. I wanted to give her more of my minutes. I wondered if her stories were imaginary ones or real ones that had somehow managed to shake loose of their trappings to be told again.

I thought about her when I went to bed that night and again when I was leaving her city the next day. I wondered about her life in Jerusalem, and I wondered how the war impacted her as a girl. I wondered about her husband. Because she told us her last name, I didn't have to look far. He was someone who was easy to find.

Turned out, most all of her stories were real.

Her husband, a Jew born in the U.S., is to this day considered a hero in Israel's War of Independence. He helped smuggle surplus World War II armaments out of America after the war ended, which made him a criminal under U.S. law and at the same time the *single most important contributor to the survival of Israel,* according to Prime Minister David Ben-Gurion. The FBI was hot on his trail during those days though, because he'd broken the law. He was eventually arrested and fined and stripped of all civil rights in the U.S., including his right to vote. Rina lived the story by his side.

"There are critical moments in history when to act morally, one may be called upon to ignore the letter of the law, and for a just cause, to choose to put one's freedom at risk. Al Schwimmer understood this."

The writer of these words was Joe Spier, Jewish historian and writer. Though he was speaking about Rina's husband, he indirectly spoke of Rina too. A husband would never engage in such a life without the collaboration of his wife. How wonderfully audacious she must have been.

President Clinton pardoned Rina's husband in 2000. Her husband never asked to be pardoned though, because he'd done the right thing. He said he worried there would be a second Holocaust if he didn't do something to help. So he did. Simple as that.

They lived most of their married life in Israel, where he passed away five years ago. It was the one part of Rina's story that wasn't real. I was sad he wasn't arriving in New York the following day, as Rina expected, but I hoped she would enjoy the Yiddish version of *Fiddler* anyway.

Though she couldn't tell me the whole story, Rina gave me a map to follow the trail. At first glance, she was a little elderly woman getting pizza. But then, she smiled at me and I smiled back and she decided to tell me some things. She was right to tell me I would see her again, because I saw a hundred little glimpses of her the next day in the writings about her husband—and more over the next weeks as I watched documentary after documentary about their lives. Though she was only mentioned a few times by name, she was there in every adventure of the whole story. Those stories were still very much alive in her mind and for some wonderful reason, they spilled out to me in a pizza joint one day. Those thirty minutes were some of the best I've ever unhanded.

New York is a million stories.

Your town and my town are millions more.

They are everywhere.

For a few days, my husband and I sauntered our way in and out of them—until bits and pieces of one of them was told to us in the last precious hours in a big city.

I often wrap my hands around my time and guard it closely. But you know what? It passes anyway. It doesn't keep. The minutes tick away and are gone, often with little to show for them. When I turn loose of my time and lay it on the table for the taking, sometimes in a pizza joint in Manhattan, an old woman named Rina will wander in and accept the gift of it. Stories that have been locked up in her mind will suddenly be remembered and she'll tell them to a stranger who reminds her of someone. She'll do it because of one thing.

Because there was time—the place where the best stories live.

Chapter 27

CROW DOESN'T TASTE LIKE CHICKEN

Turning Loose of Entitlement

I guess I assumed my baby boomer status exempted me from certain traits. Oh, make no mistake, the title comes with a plethora of characteristics all its own—ones when taken to the extreme can be horribly unattractive. We boomers can be too competitive, too goal-driven, and too disciplined to the point of an OCD diagnosis. I've owned all of these for years at a time.

But entitlement? Nope. Not my circus, not my monkey. It's a millennial problem. Come on, you guys. You have to own up to at least a *few* undesirable traits.

But like so many sweeping statements I've made in the past, the above statement will join a long list of them which have circled back around to bite me in the behind.

Here's the thing about turning loose of one thing. It leads right up to another thing, and before you know it, you've opened up a whole can of worms.

Lord, have mercy.

I'm about average when it comes to smarts. I *could* learn more about the inner workings of the cellular world if I wanted to—I have full confidence in my ability to do so. But I don't want to. I couldn't care less how a cell phone works, I just need it to work for me. I don't need the interruption of a problematic phone.

And there it is. The first whisper of entitlement.

So, my phone.

One day, it gave me the message: *Cannot take photo. You do not have enough storage. You can manage your storage in settings.*

Well, the last part of it was untrue. I indeed could *not* manage my storage in settings.

Usually, my husband handles all things phone related for me. If you judge me for this, I'll be disappointed in you. I do laundry, and he does phones. When he was too busy to tend to my problem in a timely manner, I did the grown-up thing and drove forty-five minutes to a whole other town to resolve the problem. It's where the unhanding began—or rather, where the unveiling of the thing I needed to turn loose became as evident as a third eye in the middle of my head.

There was a nervous and buzzing energy when I entered the phone store, as I looked around at all the waiting people. It immediately stressed me out. My name was taken and added to some list. I found a seat on a little pleather stool and waited exactly one-point-five hours to speak with someone who knew about phones and upgrades and stuff. I waited patiently. In fact, the sales associate kept thanking me for being so nice and patient.

"Oh please! Of course! Not a problem," I said. And I meant it. When I'm anxious and uncomfortable, I tend to be overly nice in an awkward and slightly nauseating way. Plus, I'm a middle child. I want to please.

You probably know the drill in phone stores because you've been handling your phone like the grown-up you are for some time now. Not me, though. I'm a newbie at this, having just uncurled myself from the fetal position.

So I ordered a phone.

The details of the transaction don't really matter so much as the fact that after some research when I got home, I realized one aspect of the transaction seemed a little shady to me. It smelled of scam. My imagination? Maybe. But I smelled a scam. Buyer's remorse set in.

When I called to cancel the phone I'd ordered, no person could be reached. Only machines. I tried several times. I left a voicemail and a text message with my sales associate—why don't we call him Bob. Bob, the cell phone sales associate—the one who told me I was a pleasure to do business with. I came up empty-handed with all my attempts. I got nothing. No one would talk to me. I tried to pull up the website they gave me to register my old phone for a trade-in. And here is what it said:

THIS PAGE NO LONGER EXISTS.

See? It has *scam* written all over it.

I saw a cute kitchen towel in a little shop recently. It said this:

Forgive me for the things I said when I was hungry.

I would like to take the liberty of adding an addendum to the above statement.

Forgive me for the things I said on that one particular day when I was hungry and I had to return to the cell phone store to cancel a scammy order. Yeah. Forgive me for that.

Trust me when I say it was the nastiest of nasty combinations.

Again, I made a forty-five minute drive to the phone store to cancel in person. I was already mad about it. My husband was with me because I'm weak, like I told you. I was hungry, fueled only by caffeine. We found a parking spot between the phone store and Walmart. He took off to find a headache remedy, insisting I wrap up my phone business myself.

I walked into the store with my receipt in hand to simply say, "Cancel my order, please." See how polite I planned to be? Really. That's what I meant to say. I did.

But what happened next was right out of Romans chapter seven.

I do not understand what I do. For what I want to do, I do not do, but what I hate to do, I do.

They invited me to put my name on a list, saying the wait would be forty-five minutes. That's when I told them I'd already waited one-point-five hours only a few days ago and I did not want to wait again.

"I just need to cancel my order," I said in my inside voice—calling forth my best passive-aggressive self.

The sales associate wasn't having it. He said I had to wait anyway. The entire room of people suddenly went quiet and seemed to be waiting in anticipation for my response. I did not disappoint.

"No. I won't wait. Here is my receipt," I said. "Just cancel my order."

The girl behind the counter stopped with her current customer and offered to take my number and handle it. The guy behind the counter said these actual words. He said them to her, but he looked at me with a smirk on his face as he said them.

"You can do what you want, but I would make her take a number and wait."

The customer to my right looked at me with such disdain and then she made a sound something like *phuh*. At me—the nice, patient one from a few days ago. No one had ever *phuhed* me in my life. *Ever.* My face felt hot, *and* I was hungry.

I gave the sales associate my number to cancel my order. I said thank you. I distinctly remember saying thank you, because I'm polite that way. Then, I ducked my head and turned to go.

It was the walk of shame, as I felt every eye was on me as I left. On me—the one who was busier than all of them—way too busy to take a number and wait. Too entitled.

Dear Lord, I'm a baby boomer. Surely, I don't have to turn loose the very thing I'm sure I am not.

Walks of shame always seem to happen in slow motion.

Outside, it was a cool, crisp day. I tried to turn the page by focusing on the sheer joy of rollback prices at Walmart.

Nope. Wasn't happening.

And I was still hungry.

In the car, I relived the whole sordid affair for my husband. I told him about the *Phhuhh* lady and how she directed her disgust at me.

"Can you believe it?" I asked. I kept talking and he kept listening. I was the queen of justification as I kept trying to make him see *me* as the offended one. No matter how hard I tried to spin the story in my favor, my arguments only sounded weak and pitiful in my own ears.

In the end, I circled around third and headed for home, with no other conclusion to draw except I'd behaved badly. Like an entitled spoiled child. With an audience.

"I'm not that girl," I said to my husband. "Today, you were," he said back.

I hate when he's so smart about things.

"I'm going to have to go back in there, aren't I?" He just raised his eyebrows as if to say, *It's up to you.*

I know our lunch must've been delicious, but to me, it tasted a lot like crow.

Third trip to the cell phone store.

I hoped all the customers who'd been there a few hours ago were gone, but the store was still full of people. People waiting their turns. They were nice. As opposed to me—the *not nice* one. As I walked in, the same female sales associate looked up at me with an alarming *Oh, no, not again!* look.

I quickly mouthed the words, *I'm sorry.*

She motioned for me to approach the counter. She was with a customer and she started to ask him to wait, but I quickly reached out my hand and laid it on hers before she could say anything. I apologized for my earlier impatience. I told her I should have taken a number. The guy behind the counter—the one from before—still didn't give me the time of day, but it was okay. I deserved it.

But the girl. She showed such lovely grace. She gave me her card and said I could call her personal number if I had any other questions.

Just a few hours earlier, at church, I'd silently vowed to try to go an entire day without saying one negative thing. Things sure can go south quickly.

Here's the thing about entitlement. Each of us wears it differently.

Sometimes it looks like wanting something for nothing. Sometimes it looks like thinking we deserve something, even though we haven't done the hard work or put in the time. And sometimes, it is simply thinking of oneself more highly than the next person—like self-importance. Like I'm the queen and all others are sorry people.

The latter was the flavor of entitlement I wore that day.

Unhanding an attitude of entitlement looked like this for me. First, it was coming around to the idea that my baby boomer status did not exempt me from the trait. Seeing it is one thing, but we can't fully unhand a wrong way of thinking until we set things right if the situation calls for it. For me, it was an apology. And finally, it required an intentional shift in my thinking—a retraining of an inner wiring—an installation of a check valve to detect even my slightest entitled tendency. And you know what? With continual practice, I can begin to see others as brothers and sisters walking through life alongside me. Not more than me. Not less than me. Simply, the same as me. It's hard for entitlement to live in that space.

No one likes to wait at a cell phone store. And though I was there with a problem, it's likely others were there over the top excited to be getting their very first cell phone. I'm trying to make it my habit to sit and study the room when I must wait, imagining stories of the people around me and all the ways we're alike.

You know, it would seem eating crow would leave a really foul taste in your mouth, and it does. Just for a bit. But the aftertaste is sweet … like I just brushed with Crest Triple Action Toothpaste, guaranteed to keep my breath minty fresh for up to twelve hours.

Or until the next time I have to eat crow.

Chapter 28

THINGS RECLAIMED

Turning Loose of Perfection

New and shiny things mostly don't hold my attention. I was imprint-
ed in the womb to love old, used things. My grandmother traveled
the world and collected old things—things like sideboards, pitchers,
bowls, chairs, china, chaises, and clocks. Her old oak sideboard lives
in my house now. Long before *American Pickers* told everyone junk
was cool, my mother was on the hunt for it. My sisters and I furnished
our first places with her treasures and then, carrying on the family
tradition, began to mix in some of our own finds.

My heart beats faster as I approach anything resembling a yard
sale because there's a thrill for me in things discarded. Old clocks that
don't work. Beautiful china with chips and cracks. Books with tattered
spines and beautifully faded covers. Wooden chairs with broken seats.
Mirrors with worn silver. These things live in my home. I think I'm
drawn to them because of the story of them—the stories of how they
lived before and how they became imperfect.

A small stained glass window, camouflaged by years and years of
caked-on dirt, almost got past me one day when I was on the hunt. As

I carefully rescued it from the bottom of a pile for a closer look, a lady told me she would take five bucks for it. When I pulled it out, I saw it had a few cracks and a small triangular piece of glass was missing. I would've paid ten bucks for it, but I gave her a five and took it home.

In the storeroom, I began to clean off layer upon layer of dirt, and slowly, a simple design began to emerge—a single red tulip with two green leaves. I wondered where the glass had lived in its better years. I wondered whose hands had gently cleaned the fragile panes. I wondered how it was broken and who discarded it when it became imperfect. Who decided it was imperfect? Though there were no explanations for all my wonderings, I was glad I was the one who reclaimed it.

That beautiful little piece of glass I purchased for so little money lived for many years in a window in a room where I spent time every day. The morning sun would shine through it, creating the prettiest shapes and colors despite the imperfections. It's hard for a window to go through life without them.

It's impossible for a person to go through life without them. I know it more fully with the passing of each year.

There were years when I ran hard toward perfection—when I chased after the phantom woman—the one who was perfect at every single thing. She was the very best mother, the very best wife, the very best friend, and the very best daughter. Her spaghetti was made with homemade sauce, not jarred Ragu, and her children somehow managed not to drop any of it on their clothes. She dressed well and cried pretty. She always had the perfect scripture for the occasion. She entertained flawlessly. She was the woman I tried to be.

The harder I ran toward her, the faster she ran from me, refusing to let me get close enough to look in her eyes—to learn her ways. My imperfections stood in stark contrast to her perfections and I felt less for it.

In the late 1990s, I ran out of breath. And I made a discovery.

Turned out the phantom gal was a fraud. A mirage. An apparition. Smoke and mirrors. For years, I'd measured my shortcomings against her successes. I'd clung tightly to the possibility of perfection, striving hard for it.

Striving had taken so much of my time—time I soon filled with digging around for old stuff. It's when I found the stained glass window.

It's funny how it took years of loving old imperfect things before I began to see the lesson—the point of imperfection in things and in people. While I had so much grace for an old chipped china plate—looking right past the flaw to see the delicate flower pattern—I wasn't nearly so forgiving of myself. When I learned to offer myself the same kind of grace, I saw my cracks were actually my kryptonite. When I could see the story of me as a lovely becoming, I began to see other people the same way. We're all chipped and cracked and broken in different ways and it's the beautiful mark on us of being human. We were, in fact, uniquely created to live and learn in the mess of things.

In unhanding the dream of perfection, I quit running. I caught my breath and I became a student of the imperfection in me and the imperfection in others, and I found a beautiful harmony there. I scouted for flaws. I looked deeper. I found it in an old songwriter, in a poor girl, and in a young mother who can't keep up. I find it every day as hard consequences and divine providence play out in my life and in lives all around me. I find it in the tears of friends on my back porch. It's there when I think, *I could've done better.* It's there when an old woman says, *All of it is my fault.* Being imperfect scrubs away the shine on us and replaces it with a lovely patina. We become like well-seasoned, old cast iron skillets. When you show me the chink in your armor, I begin to know you. The story of you is there. When you see the tear in me from a deep sadness, you see something real. You see no matter how I wish I could be stronger, sometimes I can't. The real story of me is there. Perfection drives us apart. Imperfection pulls us together. We are a band of imperfects—you and me. There's a beautiful light shining through the broken parts of us. I see it now.

I thumb my nose at the phantom woman every time I embrace the limits of me.

Of all the unhandings, turning loose of perfection has quite possibly had the most life-changing effect on me. I reclaimed the me that is the perfect amount of imperfection—a perfect amount of enough. The grace of it all has dusted everything in my life with a layer of lovely despite the flaws. There is a curious light filtering up from the crevices now. It fascinates me more than ever.

Once I saw my imperfection as a malformation. It wasn't. It was a *formation*. It was the beginning of being me. *Becoming* is so much sweeter than *chasing*.

Chapter 29

I'VE GONE TO SEE THE ROSES

Turning Loose of a Life

For thirty-four years, I've thought of motherhood as it applied to me. I've chronicled the ebb and flow of it—written about the continuous fine-tuning of my heart regarding the holding on and letting go of my own children.

All the while in the background, there was a letting go running parallel and concurrent to mine—a releasing very much in sync with me. It was a quiet release—a graceful one. An unselfish one. It was never written about, at least not by me, until this very moment, because only now do I see it for the lovely thing it was. And is.

I'd forgotten that to someone else, *I* was the child being continuously released. Then, in the earliest and darkest hours of Valentine's Day, my mama let go of me for the last time on earth.

For almost fifty-nine years, I had a mother. She called me Daney. Her name was Glenda Faye.

She was beautiful, and she loved me with her whole heart every day she breathed. Well, there might have been a few off days, but let's not split hairs. Even when I had my own life and grew busy in it, she loved me. She gave me space to tend to my life, and she began to tend to her pretty pink roses, because a mother's tending has to go somewhere. Where once she'd gardened me with her hands, she began to garden me with her heart—in the secret place where she could, without my knowing, pluck and pray away the weeds I didn't see growing. It's the way this motherhood thing goes down, I'm learning.

I see it now—the full circle of it. She held my hand from the minute I was born, and I held hers until the minute she was gone. The in-between was real and crazy and loving. It was gritty and alive and maddening. It broke my heart so fully the day she died, but even that was part of the whole—all of her life was one extravagant gift, the fullness and meaning of which I'm only beginning to see. Little pieces of her have been revealed to me in part every day since.

It was just like her to plant something that patiently waited to show itself until now—until she's gone. She was always good at cultivating a surprise.

All of a sudden, it was one month and some days without her.

Then, three months later.

And then, six months, and I'm unsure how it's possible that she's been absent for so long.

When I was twenty-one, I was helping Mom color her hair in the bathroom. In another room of the house, my then-boyfriend/now-husband sat with my dad. We had an inkling, my mother and I, their discussion might have something to do with a blessing to marry. There was way too much nervous energy and curiosity in that tiny bathroom that night, so Mom did the thing that came naturally to her. While Clairol honey blonde color worked its magic on her roots, she painstakingly crawled on her hands and knees through the living room to eavesdrop, looking back at me along the way as she tried to stifle her laughter, which would've totally foiled our plan.

I don't even remember the outcome of the night. I just remember Mom. The joy of her. The fun of her. It's the only way I've managed to let her go.

I remember it in the way her eighty-year-old spry self effortlessly climbed the steep stairs to my house—powered by her brown Chuck Taylors—all for a good cup of coffee and a few minutes together with me. She sowed joy in our ordinary days together. It's like she planted all these little seeds in me along the way, and they're beginning just now to break through the soil—emerging as these deeply rooted, brightly colored happy stories—all of them stitched together with her love that never waned. She'd clearly been planning it all along with every story we made together. And on the days when the stories find me again, Glenda Faye is still fully alive.

Surprise. Here I am.

I'm smiling now as I write, because I can almost hear her say those words—her slightly irreverent and always left-of-center sense of humor oozing from every letter in the sentence. It's the gift she left for me so I would smile. It's the next best thing to having her here.

I walked the block from my house to hers today. I checked the mailbox. I went inside just to make sure everything was okay. I sat at the piano for a minute. I suppose all I'm really doing is looking for her—some piece of her. I don't think it's possible to untangle the ache for her from the joy of her. It's all mixed together now. I'm waiting for something in my gut to settle down. I sat in the backyard for a bit. She would love how it's coming alive. I almost looked right past the metal sign she hung on the fence a long time ago—the familiarity of it causing me to nearly miss it. I read the scripted words written over green paint—most of it beginning to fade:

I've gone to see the roses.

And so you have, Mom. So you have. I hear they're really something over there.

It's how I let go of her—I picture her there in her garden that will soon be someone else's garden. I know the unhanding of her isn't forever. Mom's wind chime hangs in my garden now, and every time the wind picks up and I hear the music, I know it isn't the end of her. I like to think of it as her very best beginning.

Chapter 30

WHEN EVERYONE STAYED HOME

Turning Loose of the Outcome

"What do you think is going to happen?" asks everyone.

"I don't know," everyone answers back.

This is the curious conversation playing over and over around the world, pinging about as if we're all in some strange echo chamber. I sit writing a chapter I never planned to write—like a storyboard for some otherworldly science fiction movie—revealing still another opportunity to turn loose of something.

Only eight months ago, I was in Iceland. I was on a black lava beach collecting sea glass—regular old glass etched smooth by a collision of salt and sand, movement and time. My husband and I were with friends, living for fourteen days in the closest quarters—sharing tiny spaces as we traveled the entire ring around the country. It feels like a far reach in *this* moment to imagine ever returning to that place—or to most *any* place, if I'm honest.

Because there's this virus going around.

As I imagine all the possible outcomes of this thing—prognosticators have laid out a veritable smorgasbord for me—I can feel my gut clinch. I'm well acquainted with the feeling. It's my warning sign—my body's reminder for me to turn loose of all of it.

For over forty days now, every citizen in the U.S. has stayed home—*sheltering in place*, we call it, as we hope to flatten the curve of the spreading of the illness—one which we know little about and are ill-prepared to handle *if* the worst-case scenarios play out. So far, they haven't. Still, we remain vigilant and cautious.

Most all the countries in the world are doing the same, to some degree anyway. Our businesses have been forced to pause, which means many will never reopen. We're only supposed to go out for essentials like food and exercise, staying away from each other as much as possible. People are wearing gloves and masks. We're living in small pods, apart from friends and family, communicating mostly through technology. Anything antibacterial or with bleach is almost impossible to find. When we do find it, we keep it at the ready to wipe away any trace of an actual human who might contaminate us or our surroundings. And for some strange reason, there is no toilet paper. I think, perhaps, this is the oddest thing of all.

Most touches with people are gone, or at best awkward and cautious. I'm tearing up as I write these words, acknowledging how I've taken for granted all the simple nuances of human interaction—nuances unique to each person and only perceptible when we're close enough to breathe the same air. I miss this the most. I miss seeing people in 3D. I miss their full-on, no holds barred hugs.

Our government is printing money like crazy to keep us all afloat, sending out money to every taxpayer. But of course, there are glitches and requirements and paperwork. At best, it's only a bandage on a very bad wound.

Personally, I'm sheltering in my home in a rural town. Our business can survive for a while, and my husband and I are in good health. We're team players and playing it safe. Still, my jaw hurts from clinching my teeth when I sleep. We have immediate family on the front line in the medical profession, and risk of exposure is always there. We have children whose sources of income have disappeared. We miss all of them. We miss our grandchildren. We are *doers*, and we can't *do* anything. I worry. We all worry.

All of us, everywhere worry.

Because we are dangling here, and we don't know for how long.

We don't know for how long.

We want to know when it will end. We want to know when it will feel right again, and we can't know. We simply can't. We have zero control over the outcome. This very thing is hard for me to accept. My tendency is to keep rolling it around in my head—examining it from every possible angle so I can figure it all out. And I'm usually quite good at it—problem solving, that is. Ask anyone in my family, and they'll agree. But this thing has busted me. My bent is to weigh the pros and cons over and over and over—this time, to no avail at all. My fear rises and falls. My anger rises and falls. Which leads me to this.

Walk on—far, far away from the talkers. Lay it down and keep doing it again and again. It's what I've done most every day of this pandemic. Daily, I pry my fingers off my need to know the outcome by speaking aloud four words I learned as a kid:

Thy will be done.

You see, *my* agenda and *my* calendar are not the thing here. All my plans which have gone missing are not the thing here. There are things unseen by the naked eye at play in these strange days, and when I can finally settle my mind around this, I can unhand the outcome of the most fear-inducing things in this life. If I can take this in and understand this truth of it, I can turn loose, get quiet, and let things play out. Even in a pandemic. Or I can hang on tightly and let it drag me through every craggy, dark, and depressing place. My choice.

At some point almost every day, I end up down at the river that runs beside my home. Time passes as I walk and walk and walk. On desolate stretches of riverbank, I scout for river glass—the same thing as sea glass, minus the element of salt, of course. It's been my place of refuge and solace—my beauty during these uncertain days. Quite surprisingly, my teacher, too. On these walks, I'm single-minded. With every piece of river glass I pick up, it seems I lay down a little of the beast that keeps trying to steal all my joy away.

I never know the outcome of my hunts. Some days, I find brown amber glass, very common where I live. My friend calls it *beer glass,* but it's so beautiful after the river refines it. Some days, I find glass that isn't ready, meaning it's still rather sharp and transparent, so I bury it deeply in the sand so the river can rise one day and tumble it around some more to smooth out its jagged edges. Other days, I find a piece of rare cobalt blue glass, and I can't believe my good fortune.

Here's the thing. I only find glass when I'm looking ahead just as far as the next step I will take. If I begin to look beyond that space—if I widen my lens to see farther in front of me—I'll completely miss the treasure lying right at my feet. Such a simple lesson for such complicated times—to see *this*—just *this* and no more.

In just over forty days' time, my bowl of river glass is almost running over. I found each piece one step at a time. I found it, never knowing for certain I would. I found it by keeping my eyes focused on what was right in front of me. I found it without any thought for all the other pieces I *wouldn't* find. I found it by not concerning myself with the outcome.

I like to imagine the day when this is done—when these current afflictions are found to have been temporary and to have actually, in a weird way, made us better people. I like to imagine the day when our trusting and hoping comes to fruition. I pray I'll be found to have not squandered a minute of this unexpected gift of time by trying to cling to some selfish, shortsighted outcome.

I like to imagine the day when God, having brought us through this madness, looks down at earth on a sunny day and sees all of us washed up and sunning ourselves on the riverbank—a little broken from the storm perhaps, but with our jagged edges made smooth and our color made radiant.

Like river glass.

Chapter 31

GALS WITH GUMPTION

Turning Loose of Friends

When I was thirteen, I did something very mean. In the school snack bar one morning, where all the students gathered before class, I impulsively pulled the chair out from under my best friend, Ruth. She fell hard to the floor, her cheerleading skirt flying up right along with her hands, no time to brace herself for the fall. I remember there was lots of laughter. Then, I remember her disbelieving gaze that fell upon me right before she gave me a good smack upside my head with the purse we fondly referred to as *the canteen*.

Yes, I had just humiliated my best friend in front of our peers. I shudder to think I might have harbored some pent-up hostility and jealously toward Ruth, since she made cheerleader and I didn't. I was the runner-up, you see, which meant I would spend game days wearing normal clothes to school instead of a cute red and white cheerleader uniform. It also meant I would spend ballgames sitting in the bleachers with the Pep Squad (the cheerleader wannabes) dreaming of what it would be like to be out on the field with the cheerleaders who were living their very best life. Like Ruth.

Somehow, Ruth forgave me so our friendship could continue.

Ruth and I, along with our other close pals, had no idea how the daily ins and outs of our young lives were knitting us together for life. We had no idea we would one day find great joy in remembering all of our coming-of-age stories. But before we could find joy in it, we had to miss it. And before we could miss it, we had to let each other go.

I never knew when I hugged my girls and took pictures with them on graduation day, I was actually letting them go. We were young and excited for the next thing. Some of us stayed in touch for a while. One of my friends was my college roommate, but eventually, we all lost the rhythm of our friendships.

Where social media refuses to let classmates be totally out of touch nowadays, in the 1980s, most of my friends actually vanished from my life and I vanished from theirs. We'd have short visits at a few reunions, and we'd feel the beginning of our old friendships catch a breath, but then we'd disappear again for another ten years. Rose was the one who always remembered birthdays and some of us shared short, polite exchanges on Christmas cards for some years too, but not with the familiarity we'd once had. We'd each become busy in our new adult lives. There were moves and marriages, children and jobs. There were gut-wrenching seasons we never shared with each other in real time.

When I thought about it, I was sad at the twists and turns these friendships took as time rolled by. I missed the ones who knew the girl in me. I hadn't anticipated all the ways we would grow apart, and I certainly couldn't have anticipated the joy of our coming back together in mid-life. Sometimes when we turn loose, it isn't the end of the story. Sometimes there is still power to the line that was cut and all it needs is a new connection.

Thirty years after I hugged them goodbye, our class came back together for one short weekend reunion. Something was different that year with my girlfriends and me. Our lives were more settled. Our children were growing older. We were growing older and something in us needed each other again. Before we parted ways, the ten of us vowed we would have a minireunion soon. It was time.

It happened, and it has happened every year since—twelve years and counting. During all the years we were apart, unbeknown to us, an invisible, thin thread connected us until the day came when we could properly stitch ourselves back together.

Years have melted away, and because our vision has declined, miraculously, so have our wrinkles. Our diets have changed because now roughage is hugely important to our quality of life. We drink coffee *always* in excess and red wine occasionally in excess. The year we turned fifty, we had a cake for ourselves along with presents.

The first year, we talked about the things that bonded us. Things like Mr. Blackwell's government class. Kissing advice. Learning to cook in home economics class. Making the drag on Saturday nights. Liking the same guy at the same time, which is bound to happen in a small town. Choir pranks and water skiing trips and sunburns. We even remembered our *handles* on our CB radios and our nighttime drives on minibikes without lights. We howled about the spats we all had.

Everything wasn't fun and games, though, and we talked about that too in the second year.

We talked about bullying. We didn't call it out back then, but it happened. We all experienced it and we told each other what it felt like to be teased about our weight and how badly it hurt to be called *Shirley Pimple*. We took the covers off of all secrets and talked about hard home lives. We talked about how a little girl survived losing her mama. We remembered a tragedy in our town that made national news and we remembered our classmate, Clara, who died in it. We asked each other questions we wouldn't ask back then and we explained the things we couldn't mention before—when we were young, immature, and completely uncomfortable in our own skin.

Somewhere in the middle of all the years we were absent from each other, there was a lot of life that happened. We talked about all of it the third year, as we slowly remembered how much we could trust each other. We talked about getting married, getting unmarried, and getting remarried. During those years, we had babies and they grew up and some of those babies tore their mama's hearts apart for a season. We lost people we loved. We traveled. We went completely broke. We had grandbabies. We had wonderful moments and we had some really crappy ones.

But here we are. We are now all officially filled in on each other's old news. So we've turned the page.

When we meet up every year, we quickly fill each other in on cursory life updates and share any new thrilling secrets. Once all of it is out of the way, we're off and running. We go ziplining. We paint, go pumpkin picking, and go junk digging. We taste new wine, except for Lisa, who won't ever indulge in a sip. We soak in the small rapids in a spring-fed river, trying not to think about the snakes swimming with us. We meet at a different place each year and we have proven we will even ford flooded streets to get to each other.

We have a continuous text thread and we will drop everything when an S.O.S. comes down the pipe. We are a safe house for each other. We will wear rally caps for each other when needed. We have the same root system and after all these years, they are so tangled up with each other, no one gets away from us. We share a history that will never again be duplicated or spoken of, except when we are together. Thank the Lord.

We have latched on to each other with a gusto that can only come after a long separation.

Sometimes we unhand people because they have to grow on their own for a while. And sometimes, after all the growing is done and most of the life lessons have been learned, they are returned to us as one great big surprise.

Let me say this:

There is an age when we miraculously turn loose of comparison and perfection. We turn loose of taking ourselves so darn seriously. There is a place where we are all just who we are.

In this place, the joy of friendship literally explodes all over us. We've been growing into it since we were little girls playing on the merry-go-round in grade school. Fifty years later, I do believe we've settled into the best versions of us. We like us in whatever skin we decide to arrive in. We're tender with each other's secrets, accepting of each other's quirkiness, and forgiving of each other's shortcomings.

Cheers to the friends of my childhood—the gals with gumption—who came back to me years after I turned them loose. We're sixty now, and on occasion, we swim with snakes and zipline across valleys because we're tough as nails. Age is nothing.

Chapter 32

SUPPER

Turning Loose of Fancy

There was a time in my life when I wanted to be fancy.

In hindsight, I think the reason for it was because I'd always seen myself as plain and average—with zero wow effect. When I moved from my small hometown to a city, things were different there. People were a refined sort and upwardly mobile. I'd never known a million-aire in my whole life, but by the time I turned thirty, I had a friend who became one.

I made new friends who were fancy, so I wanted to give it a try. Though it didn't appear that millions would be in my future, I became very good at finding Tuesday Morning knockoffs. You know, *the look* for way less. For the first time in my life, I had a manicure. I began to use skincare and makeup products I didn't buy at the grocery store. Though I didn't know what brie was, and I'd never eaten any kind of lettuce besides iceberg, I observed and I learned. I bought beautiful things we couldn't necessarily afford because acquiring things was what everyone around me was doing. I bought things I wasn't even sure I liked, but I wanted to be like the ones who *did* like them, so I took their word for it—the fancy ones.

It was the 1980s, so popping up your collar was so fancy. Luann was someone I looked up to for her fashion style and for her beautiful home and beautiful children. She *always* popped her collar. So you *know* I had to try it. It was a Sunday morning and I walked in the church door thinking I was so couture—until right off the bat, I was greeted by a slightly older woman who said in a joyful singsong voice, "Good morning! Oh, here, let me fix your collar!" I, of course, let her fix it, feigning complete ignorance it was standing at all.

No one would dare touch Luann's popped collar, because everyone knew she meant for her collar to be that way. Because she was fancy without even trying. Let me tell you though, when you are born unfancy like me, not a single soul on the planet is going to believe I intended to wear my collar popped.

The experience discouraged me for a bit, but still I chased after fancy like the high achiever I am.

I picked an unfortunate time to try fancy, however. With two toddlers and a baby on the way, fancy wasn't happening, no matter how hard I tried. No one cooperated. Not my husband, and definitely not my little boys. Things broke, got dirty, and I was always mad about it.

Can I ever have just one nice thing? That was my mantra.

I was full-on crazy when company was coming—no matter if they were fancy people or not. If they were fancy, I wanted to appear like them. If they were unfancy folk, I guess I wanted them to see the new fancy me. I worked hard to fancy everything up in my not so fancy starter home. My family walked on eggshells—I wanted everything so perfect—as if what I'd been given wasn't enough. As if who my people were wasn't enough. Really, all it boiled down to was I didn't see *myself* as enough.

Of course, I'm only piecing all of this together in hindsight. I was in my mid-twenties, and I had no idea who I was. I had no idea of the incredible ruby *I already was.*

I'm still ashamed of my behavior back then. I tried to be fancy for so many years, but it proved to be unsustainable. Financially and emotionally. My soul was never settled in my pursuit of it anyway. And then, quite out of the blue, we moved to an old house in a little town where fancy wasn't in fashion.

That's when I began turning loose fancy. That's where I found the freedom I'd grown up with right in the middle of plain things.

When I was a little girl, supper was what we called the meal at the end of the day. When Mama opened the back door of our house and called *supper*, my sisters and I knew playtime was over and something hot and good was waiting when we came inside. I'm fairly certain Mama never had to call twice when she used the word *supper.*

It was a time when every kid in the neighborhood played outside. We were Olympic gymnasts on our swing set. We pulled the streamers out of our bicycle handlebars and inserted old keys in their place. We rode all over the neighborhood, pretending our lime green banana seat bikes were cars. We got filthy dirty as we worked up our appetites, so *supper* came to be one of our favorite words.

With very few exceptions, supper was eaten at home. Weekly staples were things like spaghetti mix from a box and something we called goulash—which, as one might guess, was a jumble of leftover things mixed in with ground beef and an insane amount of cheddar cheese sauce. Sometimes fried spam was on the menu.

Mostly, those at the table were Mom, Dad, my sisters, and me. Conversation was always lively, but my father, a man of few words, regularly spoke up when things got out of control at the supper table. We called it getting tickled—which isn't exactly the correct descriptor of the hysterics happening at the table. They could be triggered by something as simple as the configuration of green peas on a plate bearing a striking resemblance to our preacher. Or when my sisters caught me hiding the ham I detested inside the empty baked potato skin. Eventually, before things got totally out of hand, Daddy would look up and say one word in a deep, emphatic voice.

Girls!

Girls included Mama, who was always right in the big middle of it with us. There were only three rules at the table. No elbows on the table. No smacking. No television playing in the background.

What happened around our table in the 1960s and 1970s in a little oilfield town in West Texas would never be called *dinner*. Mercy, no. With dinner, there's a connotation of seriousness, with proper place settings, food, and conversation. Maybe candles and wine. People dress for dinner. At supper, as long as the hands are clean, it's good enough.

I'm uncertain as to whether families nowadays have supper. I think dinner is more in line with these times. We pick up dinner for our families because we're busy.

I'll just grab something on the way home.

We have dinner out with friends because it's easier.

Want to meet up for a quick dinner?

I find a lack of intimacy in *dinner*. We're able to keep a safe distance from each other when we meet up in public places. When we don't cook together or clean up dishes together, there is less chance we have to share ourselves. We seem to have an aversion to it. When we spill a drink at dinner, we apologize. When we spill a drink at supper, we laugh. Supper is open-ended. Dinner has a start time and a finish time. Dinner is fancy. Supper is plain.

I'm thinking about this because one day, a friend I hadn't seen in an entire year invited me to *supper*.

It's the actual word she used when she called me, and it sounded so familiar in my ear, evoking all kinds of sweet, warm images from my childhood. It had been ages since I'd been invited to *supper*.

The drive was forty-five minutes through the countryside and the minute we pulled up to my friend's house, we were greeted by her and her husband. They didn't wait for us to knock on the door, because they were looking for us. They were expecting us. We took a leisurely stroll through the century-old house they'd recently moved into—the place where generations of their family had lived. It was the house where I would be reminded of the importance of supper.

There was the time of fixing drinks together and chatting on the back porch while the food was in the oven, because supper can't be rushed. The food was simple and delicious and the table casual. Talking came easily. The conversation never waned. Laughter ensued. Later, all four of us cleared the table and rinsed the dishes together.

All of it combined—the entire night—was the definition of supper. We were four friends sitting around a table with an abundance of everything important, which turned out to be not much at all—a glass of sweet iced tea on the front end and a strong cup of coffee on the back end.

When we left, it was with goodbye hugs on the front porch under the porch light. As we walked to our car, the only sound was gravel crunching beneath our sandals, as crickets and cicadas and evening birds noisily went about their business.

With my back to the house, I heard the screen door *close* behind us. Actually, it didn't close. It *slammed*.

Of course, it did.

Because where there is supper, there is always a screen door that slams.

That supper marked the beginning of my full cooperation in turning loose of fancy—my agreement that I was my best when things were plain and simple. My joy in seeing that when I was just plain old me, I was more of everything and less in nothing at all. It was a great relief to be done with fancy. It had been an exhausting run. It was sheer delight to find plain again, exactly where I'd left it—stuffed in the back of the cabinet behind the pretty china plates and ten individual little sets of crystal salt and pepper shakers.

Simple suits me better. It suits us better, and we're happier for it. It never, ever works to try to be something we're not. It's like trying to cram swollen feet into a pair of stilettos.

So here you go, fancy—I'm done with you. I'm turning you loose, along with my solid crystal pitcher, which I'd like you to keep as a parting gift.

Chapter 33

THE WALLS THAT HELD US

Turning Loose of a Home

I sat on the floor of our old house.

It was empty then.

So many times, I'd spoken harshly about it. It was ironic that the very *oldness* that drew me to her had, over the years, driven me nuts.

Faced with the reality I would be walking out the front door for the last time the next morning, I was clinging like crazy. I was again looking at the old gal as I did the first time I saw her. And I loved her still. It was killing me to leave, even when what was waiting was so good. But it was time.

Some might find this a bit dramatic—saying, "Oh my goodness. What's the big deal? It was just a house, for Pete's sake!" Actually, it wasn't just a house. And I have so much more to say about it.

This is a tribute to the house where we grew our family—the house we all turned loose in unison. I intend to do it up right.

Twenty years ago, I picked her off a list of homes available in the little town where we hoped to move. It's safe to say she was the absolute saddest thing I'd ever seen. She was on her way to seeing better days, but someone had given up on her. They just left her there—with her boards rotting, perched above the Llano River. Just a bunch of falling down sticks, really.

When I first saw her, it was springtime. There were wildflowers all around, which softened her exterior greatly. Still, she was a mess, and it would be two years before we could actually live there. For two years, our family—my husband and I and our three children (then ten, seven, and five)—worked every single weekend, rain or shine, heat or cold, to restore the old girl. Blood, sweat, and tears. We look back on it now and wonder how we did it. We think we would never want to do it again, but there has never been a moment when we aren't glad we did.

This house fit our family like a glove. It was serendipity and blessing that led us to her. She knew us better than anyone. She knew all of our flaws and imperfections and loved us still. She saw us at our best and at our worst.

She knew our inside jokes—jokes anyone outside our family would find idiotic and halfwitted. She got them and I think they cracked her up! She knew the cheesiness we were capable of and she smiled at it. She knew our habits and routines—our rising times and our lights out times. She knew what we ate for breakfast. She knew the ways we loved each other—the ways we forgave each other. She heard a million *I love yous*. She knew our Christmas Eve anticipation, our getting ready for prom butterflies, and our college acceptance excitement. She knew our joy when one of us came home after being gone for a long time. She heard our prayers of thanks.

She wrapped her walls tightly around us when difficulties and sadness and fear came our way. She sheltered us always. She didn't try to fix things, she just listened and let us be. She was peace and quiet from the storm. She heard cries of a little girl who was afraid of bad guys and couldn't go to sleep at night. She listened as teenage boys poured all their angst and confusion into a couple of guitars. She saw pillows become wet with tears. She heard angry words we wished we could take back. She heard gut-wrenching prayers and pleas to God. She felt it when hearts broke. She shook as doors slammed. She knew intimately our most raw heartaches and pain. She carried them on her strong and competent frame and would willingly bear more for us if we would stay. But back to the joy, because it's the overriding emotion of our days lived within and around her walls.

Most times, there was so much joy and laughter, she couldn't contain it, so the windows and doors opened, and it would all spill out of them. The more people who came, the more love spilled out. And people *did* come. Families and friends and strangers. Young ones and really old ones. In fact, some traveled across the world, never planning to find shelter within her walls or food on her tables. She was a wonderful unexpected surprise for them. There were Germans and Russians and Ukrainians. Norwegians and New Zealanders. Koreans and Chinese. Ecuadorians and French. She was the best version of The United Nations, and never minded being kept up into the wee hours of the morning by lively porch conversations.

There were celebrations of all kinds. Christmases and Thanksgivings and birthdays. Mother's Days, Father's Days, and plain old days. There were people and games and good food. A few baptisms down in the river, too.

That old house was the facilitator of all of it. She never cared about being the center of attention, she was just happy to be in the background as it all happened in and around her.

I've heard it said music is what feelings sound like. If it's true, then our years in that house were ones of ongoing, never-ending feelings. Most nights, when we were all safely tucked away inside her walls, she enjoyed her own private concert—late-night serenades from our boys and our girl—songs finding their way under and around closed bedroom doors.

At times, her back porch became a stage—with an old upright piano rolled right out the door and white lights strung from her rafters. Her yard sometimes filled with as many as a few hundred new and old friends who came to listen to songs, to sit under the stars, and to listen to the river run down below.

During the day, when everyone was away at school and work, I would play her my own music on the piano and sing for her—just the two of us. I trusted her like that. I even played my old violin for her, bad notes and all.

So much music.

I, of course, feel I knew her better than anyone else. It makes sense since I spent more one-on-one time with her. I dragged furniture across her floors, I pounded nails into her walls, and I filled her kitchen with smoke more than once. I kept her clean. We were really best friends. I knew every creak in her floorboards and where those troublesome little nails were that liked to work themselves loose. I knew the way the evening sunlight poured in through her windows on the west side of the house—filtering through the trees to create the most wonderful shadow dances on the walls. I knew how she allowed the morning light to come in slowly through my bedroom windows to let me take my time waking—to ease me into the day. She was with me through ever-changing hairstyles and I was with her through quite a few paint jobs. I saw her with peeling paint, and she saw me with twenty extra pounds.

So the goodbye was hard.

Saying goodbye to a house is not like saying goodbye to a human friend. With humans, there's always a possibility, however slight, that we'll spend time together again someday. When you say goodbye to a house, it's likely for good. For always. I mean, you can drive by and look, but you can't sit within it and feel it again.

We all said our goodbyes—all five of us—a meal on the porch shared weeks before we left—when we knew leaving was imminent.

As we sat by the river, we remembered how our daughter and her elementary school friends spent hours cleaning and setting up the tree house that looked out over the river. The plan, of course, was to sleep there. I remember the giggles as they hauled sleeping bags, pillows, flashlights, radios, and snacks up the ladder and through the hatch door with so much enthusiasm. It was a great adventure until dark set in, at which time they abandoned it all for safety inside the *real* house.

The boys told of taking their paintball guns out to the sandbar in the middle of the river, where they laid on their backs and shot the guns up into the sky and at the last minute, just before the paint exploded back down on them, they rolled out of the way. Funny. Our coming together that last time was the same.

We gathered under her shadow and under the sky she and all of us knew so well. We told stories and remembered until the last possible minute. Then, just before the sadness of the moment could explode down us, we rolled out of the way. From up the hill, I believe she was listening. It was the best possible way to tell her goodbye—by remembering how fully and well we lived under her watch.

If I've learned anything in recent years, it's that we should hold things loosely. And when it's time to let go, we should make every attempt to do so with grace.

So this tribute is my attempt.

As I found myself saying the last of the last goodbyes to our old house—just before I turned loose of the key forever, I walked down the riverbank and waded out into the water. I reached my hand down to the bottom and found a rock—so refined and smooth after years of being tumbled about in these waters, which had at times been turbulent. The rock was a lot like me. I kept collecting rocks until the shirt I was using as a basket was full of them. A parting gift. I knew it was time to go.

I looked up the hill and there she sat.

If her walls could talk, I don't think she would've had words right then. And all of a sudden, I seem to have run out of them too.

EPILOGUE

I took a seat on Contemplation Rock. Oh, there was no official plaque nearby calling it that name, but it seemed the best use for the medium-sized boulder that morning, since I was in the mood to ponder some things. There was no way to know for sure, but I thought it highly likely others who'd passed by before me decided to use the rock for the same reason.

I'd headed out for a morning walk through a neighborhood in Salt Lake City, never intending to go off-road. When I reached the end of a city block, there were some rather steep stairs leading down. Without hesitation, I took them. They led to a paved walking path shaded by trees I didn't recognize—trees that weren't oak or mesquite, cedar or pecan. Eventually, the paved path turned into dirt, and I followed on. It was sometimes rocky and sometimes smooth. *Don't I know that story.* The thought humored me, likely because I was currently sailing through very smooth waters.

Spring comes much more slowly in Utah than in Texas, but on *that* morning, it was working hard to arrive. On the shaded path, I could still feel the vestiges of a greedy winter wanting more days than had been ordained it. Chill bumps rose on my arms when I reached the banks of the creek at the canyon and took a seat on Contemplation Rock.

It was mostly quiet until a soaking wet Border Collie came bounding down to me out of nowhere, carrying a stick and wearing a hopeful look. Her owner quickly called her back. In the canyon, there's a high value on peace and quiet.

So I began to contemplate. The rustling leaves. The discarded, empty pack of Camel cigarettes. I contemplated the budding green leaves silhouetted against the brilliant blue sky. I contemplated the hill just across the creek, covered in a tall, feather-soft grass—I imagined its gentle swaying motion to be a dance to Willie Nelson's "Blue Eyes Crying in the Rain." I wondered if Willie was even a thing in Utah. I didn't know, but it was my contemplation after all, so I didn't edit Willie out.

When I was younger, I contemplated other things. Heavy things and happy things. Sad things and important things. Blown out of proportion things—most all of them completely out of my control. Yet, I thought and planned and schemed how to eliminate the terrible things and replicate the happy ones. I tried to please and compromise and forgive and pretend. I strived and strived. I tried to be Wonder Woman, except blonde. The realization of it all had been in a state of becoming for some time—for some years, even—but finally, while sitting on that rock, I began to connect the dots.

Everything resolved when I opened my hands. *Everything!*

I sat there, having turned loose of so much in my life. I sat smack dab in the middle of white space—in the epicenter of *dead air*. I worked in radio for many years, and occasionally, someone would yell out, "Dead air!" and we all entered into panic mode until programming resumed. In the quiet space atop Contemplation Rock, there wasn't a single reason to rush around in a panic. There was little for me to tend there. I'd learned a thing or two after all. When things appear to be diminishing, they're actually expanding. When I turn loose, I find more. Et cetera.

I looked at my hands. My fingers were all accounted for—I'd not lost a single one of them, even after all the prying them off things. Not a single scar to be seen, just a bunch of well-earned age spots. My heart beat slowly and I was acutely aware of the peace of it all that comes from holding on loosely. From turning loose and immediately seeing something else.

At one point, I noticed the pristine, clear stream at my feet begin to run muddy. I wondered what had gotten it all stirred up somewhere upstream. The younger version of me might've sat on the bank for hours, worrying and willing it to become clear again. After all the turning loose, though, it's mostly no longer my way. I don't have to figure things out. I don't *want* to figure it all out. The admission of it felt good and right and honest. So, I got up, situated my funky white sunglasses on my nose, and turned away, knowing the stream would clear up on its own without any help from me. Because it always, always does. Dissonance eventually resolves.

The main path was in front of me, wide and smooth—the one most traveled and scattered with people here and there. But just to the left and traversing across the side of the steep hill was an interesting narrow path. I wasn't sure what was up there or if I could even climb it, but I decided to give it a go—to try to see something else. Lucky for me, I was wearing the right kind of shoes.

"Earth's crammed with heaven,
And every common bush afire with God;
But only he who sees, takes off his shoes."

—Elizabeth Barrett Browning from *Aurora Leigh*

ACKNOWLEDGMENTS

Deepest thanks to the people in the pages of these stories. Most of them have no idea how the most miniscule intersection of their lives with mine impacted me deeply in ways I will never forget. They helped me to see something. Thank you to Larry Carpenter for giving this book a publishing home. To Shane Crabtree and the team at Carpenter's Son, thank you for holding my hand the whole way through the process. To Tiarra Tompkins, thank you for editing my words in a tender way. Chyna Mason, thank you for perfectly summing up the heartbeat of the book in the dream of a cover you designed. Rachelle Gardner, thank you for your invaluable coaching, inspiring me to take this book all the way to print. To Cindy Birne, thank you for your expertise and enthusiasm in getting the word out about this little book. To Lisa Atkins, one of my Gals with Gumption—thank you for staying after me to send you pages for four years and for giving this book the very first complete read. Of course, I am so thankful to the people who are in just about every line of this book in one way or another—my family. Thank you to my husband Todd, for living fun stories with me and for giving his blessing to talk about our hard stuff; and to my children, Adam, Jake, and Lainey, for hanging tightly with us always and for teaching us much about holding on and turning loose.

A long time ago, a rather serious creative writing professor at the University of Texas gave a priceless critique to a piece written by a 21-year-old student from a tiny town in west Texas. His name was Thomas Finch. I don't know where he is in this world now, but I owe him much gratitude for seeing the writer in me. Because of him, I never doubted I could tell a story if I wanted to.

ABOUT THE AUTHOR

Dana Knox Wright has called Texas home all her life. She moved from the west Texas desert to the rolling hill country to attend the University of Texas in Austin where she earned a degree in Journalism/Public Relations. After retiring from a career in radio voiceover and copywriting, she authored a children's book, *A Pigeon's Tale* (2013), and *Saving Stories: Afternoons with Darrell* (2017). She has three grown children, two daughters-in-law, four grandchildren who call her Dovie, and an English Mastiff named Pearl. She and her husband Todd reside in the small town of Llano, Texas and enjoy spending summers in northern New Mexico.